WILL THEY

ESCAPE?

WHAT I LEARNED ABOUT TEAMWORK
WATCHING OVER 1,500 ESCAPE ROOMS

DANIEL HUIET

Book cover and interior design and typesetting by Lisa Von De Linde of LisaVdesigns

ISBN: 978-1-7352742-3-2
ebook ISBN: 978-1-7352742-2-5
audiobook ISBN: 978-1-7352742-0-1

Printed in the United States of America

First Edition, 2020

CONTENTS

Introduction

You can hear the police sirens screaming from outside the building, as the hairs on the back of your neck stand straight up. You are so focused on your task at hand, you don't even feel or notice the sweat beads slowly rolling down your face. Every team member in the group of accomplices plays a specific role in this mission, and team members are currently scattered around the room working diligently. Your job is to open the safe and get the loot. The vault is now directly in front of you. The moment you've been preparing for is finally here. All that needs to be done is to insert the four combinations of numbers to crack and open the safe, and a lifetime of ease, bliss, and vacation is yours. Behind you an accomplice shouts out the combinations and instructions to the safe. "Turn the dial counterclockwise four times landing on 72, now clockwise three times stopping on 84, counterclockwise again two times reaching 53, now for the final spin, turn the dial clockwise stopping on 87." You follow the instructions to a tee, knowing you are almost in the safe, moments away from victory, moments away from riches. Boom! A loud noise echoes down the hallway! A smashing of the front doors' downstairs and a rush of footsteps can be heard racing towards your location. The law enforcement has entered the building. They'll be at your position in less than a minute. You don't have much time but not much is needed. A simple turn of the lever will open the safe, changing your life forever. The time has come to finish the job. With your right hand you turn the lever towards the left, but nothing happens. Trying not to panic, you attempt the lever again. Nothing. Frantically you grab the safe combination from your fellow accomplice. Counter-clockwise 72, clockwise 84, counter-clockwise 53, counter-clockwise 87. At that point, the door busts open and the SWAT team bursts into the room, guns drawn. "Hands up, don't move!" they yell. Your arms are now handcuffed behind your back as a law enforcement agent escorts you to their van. You and your team are going to jail for a long time.

What happened? Prior to the heist, the team spends weeks going over the details. The who, what, where, when, why, and how were all covered in great length. Each team member knew his or her roles and what was expected of him or her. In the hustle of the moment one simple mistake was made: an error that would forever alter all of the team members' lives. The last turn of the dial was supposed to be counterclockwise not clockwise. This small miscommunication resulted in the team of bank robbers, including you, being thrown in prison for a long time. Everyone was just moments from a successful robbery but will now spend the next several years staring at those cold rods of steel in their jail cell. Of course, this story didn't happen at a real bank; it occurred at my escape room in Beavercreek, Ohio. However, the end result is what happens in several of the escape rooms I've watched over the course of three years at the business a partner and I own, called Great Escape Game: one small miscommunication costs the success of the team.

CHAPTER ONE

What is an Escape Room?

"Fear not the unknown.
It is a sea of possibilities."

−TOM ALTHOUSE−

The first question people always ask is "What is an escape room?" An escape room is a themed space at an actual physical location where you must solve puzzles, crack codes, and find hidden objects to achieve a set goal. The overall task for each room is completely different and based on the theme of the room. For example, in Great Escape's Bank Vault room, you must collect all the loot and escape before getting arrested. In our Western Saloon room, you need to find the deed to the saloon and get out of town before the prospector and his men get back. Each of the rooms is also decorated to coincide with the theme. Our Egyptian Tomb room has hieroglyphics on every wall, a gold painted ceiling, huge columns, an eight-foot statue, and the sarcophagus of the pharaoh in the room. I even flew to Egypt to make sure the details in the room were perfect. The idea is to make you truly feel as though you are in the scenario that the room is portraying. At Great Escape, every single puzzle, clue, poster, prop, and object is related to the specific theme of the room. If you are playing Great Escape's Virus Outbreak room, you will encounter science and medical-related puzzles and clues that you would easily find in an actual medical laboratory.

The idea of an escape room might sound intimidating, but I promise it's more fun than it is nerve-racking. You won't need any prior knowledge going into any of our rooms. The unique aspect of playing an escape room, especially one of ours, is that it takes all kinds of people to complete the game. Within each room there are different puzzles and clues that require various parts of the brain to solve. When a group of individuals enters a room, puzzles that are easy for one person may be difficult for another, and vice versa. This experience is true even for me. When I play an escape room, my mind works in a very specific way that is great at solving certain things and not so good at others. This is accurate with regard to nearly everyone who comes to Great Escape.

Each of our rooms holds up to eight individuals and is perfect for small or large groups. You work as a team to escape the room while the clock is ticking down from 60 minutes. Escape rooms are great for groups of friends, families, birthday parties, and work events. Escape rooms are something that almost all ages can enjoy. It's a social thing to do on any night of the week that is fun for all ages. You have one goal at Great Escape: escape the room in under one hour, which, I'll refer to at times as "winning"; "losing" will refer to failing to escape the room in one hour. The best part of the escape room is everyone must put their phones away and interact with each other in person. While these challenges are a lot of fun, they can add a lot of pressure as well.

OBSERVATION 1

Experience something new often.
You might have a little fun in the process.

CHAPTER TWO

How the Mind Works When There is Pressure in a Situation

"Pressure busts pipes,
but pressure makes diamonds."

–EARL BOYKINS–

Escape rooms can be stressful situations. Before you enter an escape room you have no clue what the inside of the room looks like, how the puzzles are setup, or how much detail the room has. The puzzles and clues are a complete mystery, and nothing can prepare you for the pressure you will feel once that timer starts. Although the difficulty of the room is defined before you enter, a sense of anticipation can sometimes overwhelm you. I know from personal experience there are times where my heart starts to race prior to entering an unknown adventure such as an escape room. This excitement and energy can be a wonderful feeling to have; however, too much exhilaration and anxiety can cause your brain to nearly shut down and almost stop responding to the challenge at hand. This shutting down of the brain happens to me, teenagers, adults, men, women, people who want to win, and—as you'll read later in this chapter—even doctors.

A prime example of buckling under pressure occurred one day when two groups from the same organization arrived to play escape rooms. One of the groups was set to play the Bank Vault, and the group I was monitoring had selected the Virus Outbreak. Both the groups were to start at the same time, and a little bit of competitive smack talking between both sides was present in the lobby. We put the Bank Vault group in first, and then I escorted my group into the Virus Outbreak. Game flow was somewhat slow with my group, which was struggling early on. This didn't set up the group members mentally for a strong finish, and halfway through the game I noticed a lady trying to force open a red medical bag that was in the room. I got on the microphone and told her she didn't need to pry anything open, at which point she set the red bag down. A minute later she was trying to force the red bag open again. I got on the microphone and asked her to please stop and reminded her that nothing in the room needed to be pried open. After my prompt, she set the red bag down for a second time. A seemingly brief moment passed by and for the third time she had the red bag in her hand trying to pry it open! I couldn't believe it. Just minutes prior to this third attempt, I had clearly told her twice over the speaker in the room to stop trying to pry open the bag, not to mention that prior to the game starting, I had covered the rules of no prying or forcing things open. Yet, she was attempting to pull this bag apart again. I once again picked up the microphone and told her to stop. She was not listening to me and kept pulling apart the red bag. Finally, the zipper holding the contents inside gave way and revealed the medical vials that would be used for the next task.

Why didn't she listen to me? I was practically yelling at her to stop, but she didn't pay any attention to my warnings. The group ended up losing badly and afterwards I got a chance to speak with the woman about her actions in the Outbreak room. She didn't seem to have any remorse and told me "she had to win." She spent more time trying to find shortcuts than actually playing the game. Ultimately, that type of thinking cost the group the win. In this case, she couldn't take the pressure and burst like a pipe that had been frozen.

The Virus Outbreak is one of Great Escape's hardest escape rooms to solve. It involves a wide variety of puzzles and tasks that require multiple thinking patterns from the active participants, making it one of the hardest experiences for players to attempt with only two people. The Virus Outbreak also offers one of its hardest puzzles Great Escape has which can be found towards the end of the experience. When you get to this puzzle, you typically have around 10 minutes left to solve and finish the final Virus Outbreak game. Sounds like plenty of time, right? It should be; however, this last task of the room is a complex three-part puzzle. Once you understand what you are looking for, the first two parts are straight forward, and most groups get past those two parts of the puzzle within five minutes. It's the last part of that game that requires some complex thinking. You might be thinking to yourself, "So what? All escape rooms require some level of complex thinking," and you'd be right; however, the timing of when you arrive to this difficult challenge is what shuts down the minds of even some of the best escape room artists. Everyone in the group knows the end is near. Humans only have a limited amount of willpower, and as participants get tripped up throughout the experience, this willpower and ability to focus breaks down. This puts an additional level of stress on people that is almost indescribable yet painfully obvious to observe when watching an escape room from the game master's perspective.

In a memorable example, I watched a group of players playing their first escape room. Within that group there were a variety of skill sets and professions, one of which was a medical doctor. The game doesn't require previous medical knowledge, but if you have it, then you will be a lot better suited to beat the difficult puzzle at the end. The group was doing well and was working on the last puzzle with about five minutes to go. The last step was too complicated for the group, and it had medical-related clues; so, group members called the doctor over to see if he could finish it. Once the doctor got the puzzle sheet in his hand, someone in the group yelled, "Less than five minutes!" On a side note, yelling the time left in your game before you die of a deadly virus usually adds more stress to the individuals playing the game, and, in general, does not help. Anyway, the puzzle has to do with blood types and the third portion of the three-part game is written in a way that isn't straight-forward. You must look at it from a bird's-eye view to understand what it is saying. Players almost always read it on the surface and don't try to figure out what it's really asking you to solve due to the rushed nature of when they arrive to it. On top of that, the puzzle is in a wall cabinet, and for the only time in the game, everyone is huddled around one spot unable to see what the people in front can see. This puts even more stress on the person, or two, that are trying to figure out the last part of the puzzle. The doctor was not immune to this stress.

Even though he had five minutes left in the game, his brain shut down. The habits his brain had formed might have been useful for surgery or other crucial skills in the medical field, but it wasn't programmed for this kind of challenge. It was a stressful time and all eyes were on him. This was unchartered territory for the doctor, and the clock was ticking. Five, four, three, two, one. Time's up! The group had failed. I walked into the room where everyone was laughing over their failed attempt to escape. Everyone, that is, except for the doctor who just stood there staring at the piece of paper in his hands. I took a couple of moments to explain how to find the last number they needed. Everyone gave their best "ah-ha" out loud, and the doctor shook his head, acknowledging he now understood how to get there. He was so disappointed in himself. I'm sure he'd been in more stressful situations than an escape room and that he had performed his job to the best degree possible; however, this was a different kind of stress. The brain develops automatic responses to habits it has created during a lifetime, and his brain had never experienced this before. In the last five minutes of the game his mind shut down and knowing the exact time in which failure would occur, he couldn't recover from it. Even the best among us can suffer from a small amount of pressure. Once again, the pipe had burst.

OBSERVATION 2

Understand how you function under pressure so that you'll be prepared for it in the future. You can't be successful if you can't handle pressure.

CHAPTER THREE

Self-fulfilling Prophecy; Think Your Way to Success or to Failure

"Whether you think you can,
or you think you can't,
you're right."
—HENRY FORD—

Often in our escape games there are two or more groups of people that don't know each other in one room. This happens because each room holds up to eight individuals, and on busy nights, two separate groups that want to play at the same time could potentially be sharing a room. These mixed teams have a similar win/lose ratio when compared to rooms where everyone knows each other. However, one thing that has stuck out to me when it comes to combined teams. Those who go into the rooms with a negative mindset about having strangers join their group will lose more often than they will win. The teams that welcome strangers into their now shared experience will win more times than lose.

I remember one group of adults—with members probably in their thirties—that was waiting in the lobby for their game to start. We told the group members that two other people who had previously reserved spots would be joining them to play the Outbreak room. One of the women in the group was very irritated by the fact that there were going to be other people trying to find the virus antidote with them. She proclaimed to anyone that would listen to her that she didn't want to play with anyone outside of her group. We'll call her

Ms. Stranger Danger. I tried to explain the potential benefits of having more people in the room, but Ms. Stranger Danger wasn't buying any of it. The two remaining players showed up shortly after this discussion, and everyone was ready to begin. If there are strangers playing a room together, I make them introduce themselves before taking them inside their escape room. I also explain that escape rooms are won by excellent communication, and it's vital to the success of the group if everyone connects well amongst each other. The players in each group introduced themselves, I went over the rules to the game, and then I put them in the room.

Game play progressed at a normal rate, and everyone was chipping in. I did start to notice that the woman who initially didn't want anyone else in the room with her group, Ms. Stranger Danger, wasn't talking with the stranger couple her group had just met 15 minutes prior. On two occasions, this apparent, or maybe subconscious, refusal to communicate with the strangers had an impact on the game and cost the entire group precious minutes.

The first occasion of no communication occurred when one member of the stranger couple said she noticed a locked box with a big red dot on it, and her comment fell on deaf ears. Later in the game, Ms. Stranger Danger found a red key. She looked around both rooms trying to find what the key opened but couldn't figure it out. She then placed the key down near where she found it. A minute went by before the stranger woman, who'd found the box earlier, found the red key and knew exactly where it went. Had Ms. Stranger Danger said she'd found a red key or listened when the girl noticed the red dot on the locked box, they could have easily saved one or two minutes. In escape rooms one minute can mean the difference between winning and losing.

A comparable situation occurred toward the end of the same game. When entering the Outbreak room there is a monitor on the tabletop toward the left. This monitor cannot turn on until players access the second room. The other member of the stranger couple, a man, made a statement out loud that maybe there would be a way to turn on the monitor. Later in the game, such an opportunity arose. Ms. Stranger Danger had found the button on the wall that said, "monitor" and pushed it. This monitor control was in the second room but turns on the screen in the first room. Ms. Stranger Danger hit the button, and nothing happened—nothing she could see anyway. In the first room the monitor turned on, but no one had noticed. She hit the button again, which turned off the monitor in the first room that she had just turned on. Thinking the button meant nothing she walked away. She did this without telling the stranger man who was looking for a way to turn on the monitor in the beginning of the game. Luckily for them, they asked for a hint shortly afterward that helped them solve the mystery of the monitor, thereby not losing much time.

Overall the stranger couple solved a good portion of the puzzles throughout the game, and it looked as though both groups would emerge from the Outbreak as winners. With 10 minutes left in the game the group was exactly where it needed to be. Seven minutes left. Four minutes left. One-minute left. Dead. The game was over. The group had failed. The group had all of the puzzles completed but ran out of time opening the last lock box, which would have given the group the doctor's radio frequency identification (RFID) card to escape the laboratory in time. All that was needed was one extra minute. Sixty seconds would have given them more than enough time to come away victorious. Just one minute. After the game the entire group went out to the lobby to get its picture taken.

The stranger couple left, leaving behind the original group, and thanked me for the experience. I stood there and talked to the original group for a couple of minutes after the entire group had "died of a deadly virus." The group's members were disappointed that they had lost. I told them how close they were and ensured them that they did an excellent job. Just before leaving the building, Ms. Stranger Danger looked at me and said, "We would have won if it was just us," and then walked out of the door. In her mind she didn't want the strangers there, and that was evident by watching her body language and lack of communication throughout the experience. I hate to say that Ms. Stranger Danger's displeasure of having outsiders in the room with her had consumed her thoughts, causing them to lose, because that might be a little over the top. However, one thing is for certain, she didn't want them in there and undoubtedly didn't want their input. In the end, and in my opinion, it was Ms. Stranger Danger's attitude towards the strangers that cost them the game. She had thought that they would do worse with strangers in the room, and, therefore, they did.

Life can be funny sometimes and often even a little ironic. Every now and then the universe throws out a test to see if we are paying attention and, on this occasion, I was. This universal check occurred exactly one week after the stranger couple and Ms. Stranger Danger's failed attempt at the Outbreak, when two groups that didn't know each other played the same room. It was déjà vu. There were four individuals ready to play the Outbreak, and I had informed them that there were going to be two more people in the room with them. I sometimes dread telling groups this because on some occasions they can get rather upset, just like Ms. Stranger Danger did. However, this group was different. After I told group members that there would be two more players joining them, a woman from the group responded with "Cool!" We'll call her Ms. Social Butterfly. Moments later, the two strangers arrived and checked in at the front desk. I went over my speech about group communication and had the two groups' members introduce themselves to each other. Ms. Social Butterfly proclaimed her excitement to the strangers and told them she was glad they were joining them and that they needed all the help they could get.

Just like the previous group with the stranger couple and Ms. Stranger Danger, things progressed at a decent pace. Here's where it got a little weird. A woman in the stranger couple said there was a red dot on a locked box. Moments later Ms. Social Butterfly found a red key, at which point she immediately handed the red key to the stranger woman and said, "You saw something red right?" The stranger woman took the key and walked over to the box and opened it. Earlier in the game, the other member of the stranger couple, a man, stated that they might be able to find a way to turn on this monitor. Ten minutes later, Ms. Social Butterfly found the monitor button. She then turned around, tapped the stranger man on the shoulder, and pointed out this button to him. She then stated, "This might help you figure out the monitor." He hit the button twice, which turns the monitor on and then back off, but this time he went into the first room and another member of the group hit the button. The monitor had been turned on. Most importantly, little-to-no time was wasted from a lack of communication.

The group went on to beat the Outbreak with more than seven minutes left, which is quite the accomplishment for a room with only a 15 percent pass rate. After the celebratory end of the game picture, Ms. Social Butterfly thanked the couple for helping the whole group so much. The stranger couple thanked everyone as well and somewhat seriously said they should trade numbers, that way when they play the next escape room, they'll be able take on the next journey as a now united team. How awesome is that?! It was probably one of the most surreal experiences I've had at Great Escape, minus the ghost in the Outbreak room—don't worry I'll tell you about the hauntings later in this book! Two nearly identical scenarios in the same room and the same problems occur within a week. The only difference was the attitude each set of teams had about each other before they began. If the team members thought it was bad to be with strangers, then they increased their likelihood of failure and miscommunication. If they didn't mind, or even embraced being with strangers, they passed more often or, at minimum, performed with fewer mistakes. Not only did the welcoming groups pass more often, but from what I've observed, they seemed to have a more enjoyable time than groups that weren't as welcoming.

OBSERVATION 3

Positive thinking will lead you
in the direction of positive results.

CHAPTER FOUR

A Group's Thought Process Before It Goes into a Room Often Determines Its Success

"The strongest factor for success is self-esteem: believing you can do it, believing you deserve it, and believing you'll get it."

—JOHN ASSARAF—

Escape rooms are a blast. I enjoy them so much that in a very short time after I had opened my escape room, I had played most of the escape rooms within an hour of my location. I had to start branching out slowly into other cities that were further away to play something new. One day my business partner, my daytime manager, and I, decided to go to Indianapolis, Indiana to play some escape games. We played two games in downtown Indianapolis and then went to another business about 20 minutes away. We won both experiences at the first location and were feeling rather confident about our abilities.

At the second escape room business, we started off by playing a Revolutionary War room. This was a fun room that had an incredible amount of detail in the props, and the room itself wasn't short on interesting arrangements. This revolutionary experience wasn't too challenging for us, and we easily beat the game with 20 minutes left. We decided to play one more before we made the trip back home. This room was a World War II experience. In this scenario, we were American captives in a German prison camp and found ourselves with a one-hour window to escape to freedom. We were excited to play the game as the theme appealed to all of us. Before the game master put us in the room, we asked him what the escape rate was. Big mistake on our end. He told us the escape rate was less than one percent. I thought to myself that couldn't be right; so, I questioned him again about it.

I am a strong believer that anyone can do and accomplish anything in life he or she sets his or her mind to. This is true especially when it comes to beating an escape room with two other guys that are good at playing them. However, after our game master told us about the less than one percent pass rate, our hearts sank. For a moment, my unwavering self-esteem and willpower gave way. We gave up on ourselves before the time even began.

Throughout the game we would find cool props and instead of focusing 100 percent on winning, we would find ourselves playing like kids with all the cool features the room had to offer. We knew we were failing before the game even started; so, we might as well get the best out of it and have fun during our hour. At the end of the 60 minutes, the door to the room opened as the game master came walking in. We had failed. We would not be escaping our World War II prison camp. No glorious end of game picture showing the human race how good we were. The game master was kind of shaking his head and told us we were one puzzle away and that's the closest he's personally seen anyone get from beating the room. Wait, what? We were close? Although he had no reason to lie, I didn't believe him. Less than one percent of the groups who enter this room, complete it. Failure was almost guaranteed. I asked if he would show me the ending, which he obliged. He wasn't lying. We had one puzzle to solve, and we would have won the game. Less than three minutes is all we needed to ensure success.

What we didn't realize was, some of the puzzles that we solved in that room were easy for us but hard for most other people. We were flying through these games without even realizing it and skipped a sizable portion of the challenges in the beginning of the prison. We didn't believe we could do it; so, we didn't bother giving it our all. We failed because that little voice in our heads that told us if no one else could do it, then neither could we. If we would have believed in our abilities, we very well could have been the less than one percent who successfully made it through that game and most likely would have set a record for the room, but we didn't. It was a humbling and eye-opening experience.

Although this story is about me playing an escape room, I have noticed on several occasions that people playing my rooms have the same experiences and reactions to hearing the escape rate and have acted in a similar manner as I did. When people ask me what the difficulty of a room is, and I tell them 10 percent chance to pass, it can either motivate them to no end or defeat them before they start. Those groups that say, "Challenge accepted" before hearing a small escape rate have a much higher chance of escaping. I will never doubt myself again, but it did make me think about something very important. Are there times in life when we question ourselves and our abilities to succeed, don't put in the effort, only to realize later that we were more than capable?

OBSERVATION 4

Believe in yourself, always.

WILL THEY ESCAPE?

CHAPTER FIVE

Don't Judge a Book by its Cover

*"Everybody is a genius. But if you judge a fish by its ability to climb
a tree, it will live its whole life believing that it is stupid."*

—UNKNOWN—

I've seen a wide variety of groups come through my escape game business. Out of all the assortment of groups and teams to come out to play, one specific week stuck out from the rest. For several weeks a gentleman was asking if he could book three rooms and watch each of the games with us in our game master area. I didn't like the idea of someone being back in our control room seeing the behind the scenes of our business. However, this gentleman was very persistent on us allowing him in the game master room to watch the groups he wanted to book. After four or five attempts on his part, I agreed to let him watch the players, and he booked three rooms with us to play on a later date.

Days later, and before the games were played, I would learn that the three groups consisted of students that were finishing their medical degrees. Everyone that was to play in the rooms was a potential surgeon, and this was their final test. Inside the room was a "mole"—someone that was placed there to observe them in person. This was in addition to the gentleman in the game master room that was watching with the Great Escape Game staff and me. All the students in the rooms were incredibly smart, sharp individuals. There is no question that any one of the students was more than qualified to perform the necessary duties that their potential new employer demanded of them. However, one test remained, and that was to determine how everyone interacted with each other. Communication in the operating room is a must. There are dozens of studies, in numerous cases in hospitals throughout the world, that show that miscommunication is not only a problem but can be deadly.

The games got underway, and I was surprised to see a lack of progress in all three rooms. There was some pressure on our part as well because the hiring manager was in the game master room with us and spent money to administer his final test to the students. Truth be told, all three groups would have failed miserably had we not given them hints with more information than we normally do. Two of the groups barely passed with some extra help from their game masters, and one of the groups failed badly.

Within each group there was one student that was the smartest academically in his or her class, yet in the escape room he or she wasn't communicating with the other players well, or sometimes at all. I remember one potential surgeon the employers had their eye on, and we watched that individual very closely. They told me point blank this individual was the smartest candidate in all three rooms and that this person was in the room I was watching. For the sake of being anonymous, I won't tell you which room that was. I will tell you that the room was beatable though. This candidate had a near perfect memory and flawless grades. This potential surgeon was the best of the best, except for one problem: this individual didn't play well with others. I observed the individual very closely while they tried to escape the room. The potential employers were right. This individual didn't talk to the others once during the game. Even when the individual discovered something or solved a puzzle, the player just continued playing without notifying anyone of what was just accomplished. It was almost as though this individual was in the room by themselves.

In the operating room, communication with physicians, nurses, anesthesiologists, and others is extremely important. This skill, or lack thereof, could potentially be the difference between life and death. After the employers reviewed the students playing the escape rooms, they had seen enough to make the final decision on which three out of the 20 students they would hire. Such a big decision that would affect the rest of their lives came down to who was the better communicator, not who had the biggest brain or highest IQ.

The next day a group of realtors booked four rooms. I had a good feeling about these realtors and was sure they would pass the experiences handily.

Almost all the realtors were dressed well, drove nice vehicles, and spoke well. The players were already organized into their respective groups when they arrived, making my life easier, and were all on time. We started all four groups close together, and we were off to the races. What happened next was one of the most painful hours I have ever had to endure at the Great Escape Game. None of the members in each group were talking to their fellow group members. There was a complete lack of communication between everyone playing. Three of the groups failed miserably and barely got halfway through the game. The group I was watching was the last to go in. It was down to me to get at least one of the four groups—this last group—to pass. If any of these groups were going to succeed, I would have to do something about it. I would give this group extra hints with the hope of getting them out. We've never had four out of four rooms fail before, and I didn't want this to be the first time.

I can't even remember how many hints I gave my group, but I know it was a lot. The group was at the end of the game and needed one more part of the puzzle to finish the game. The players couldn't get the number and weren't making any progress. The clock was ticking, and the timer was almost at zero. I kept trying to help them progress, but to no avail. Finally, the thought of all four groups failing was unbearable to me, so I simply told them the last number that they needed to win the game. Nothing happened. I heard myself in the room tell them the code, and none of the players did anything; so, I told them the number again. Still nothing transpired. They didn't hear me until the third time I told them the answer. They passed with three seconds left to go. I know most of you reading this are probably thinking that I shouldn't have given them the last answer or extra hints. Looking back, I agree that I probably shouldn't have helped them as much as I had, but in the moment, I felt terrible for them. I was shocked, to say the least.

I was a realtor myself for a couple of years in my early twenties and learned quickly the importance of communication. As a realtor, I had to understand what my clients were expecting of me and what they were looking for to guide them to make the right decision. One of the best leaders I ever met in my life was my real estate partner, Ed Thornhill. I have never had as much respect for anyone I have worked for or with as I did for him. His communication skills were some of the best I've ever seen or may ever see in my life, which was more than I could say for the players of these four groups. We told them they did great and that the first time playing an escape room is the toughest, which is true. The realtors left, and my fellow game masters and I were staring at each other wondering what the hell just happened.

Later that week, we had another different corporate party arrive. The group was a part of the Dayton branch of a national tire shop chain. The business had booked four of our rooms, and enough of their employees arrived on time for their four already organized groups to begin. Several of the team members were covered in tattoos—some of them even having neck and face tattoos. The mechanics had dirty hands from working on cars. My business partner's brother is a mechanic, and I respect the trade and the work they do. However, and I hate to admit this, I didn't have grand expectations of these players. I didn't necessarily think they would do poorly, but I wasn't expecting them to set any records or anything crazy like that. Boy, was I wrong.

Two of the groups nearly broke the record in their respective rooms, and one group did break the record. The last group failed, but barely, and only because half of the group couldn't get off work in time and arrived mid-game. The players that didn't pass were playing Area D, which is our hardest room at 10 percent escape rate, and were only two minutes away from passing. I was blown away. The communication in the rooms was on par with the best I've ever seen. There were no egos in the rooms, no know-it-alls, and no distractors. They nailed it. One would think that after blowing through our rooms they would be cheering, high fiving, and displaying a general sense of enthusiasm. This was not the case. Every single one of the players were relaxed and acted as if nothing had happened.

We gathered all the individuals and got a group picture of the four teams together. When we have big groups like that come through, we always wait until all the rooms have ended and then we get a group photo of all the players combined in the lobby. This picture is fun to take, and we usually get the winners to give us thumbs up and the losers to give thumbs down or different variations of fun photos. After the picture, I stressed again to the groups how amazing they all did and reminded the players that two of the teams almost set records in the rooms and one of the groups did set a record. None of the players seemed to react to this in the way I expected them to. They all smiled, thanked me, and were on their way. I was more disappointed in myself by judging them than I was excited that they passed. It was a humbling experience. I hate to admit that I didn't give them as high of chance of winning as the realtor or surgeons, but I didn't. How often do we judge books by their covers? How many times do we find ourselves assuming that someone is capable or not capable simply by the way he or she looks? I hope I never make that mistake again.

OBSERVATION 5

Don't judge a book by its cover.
Everyone is an expert or good at something.
It's your job to find out what that is.

CHAPTER SIX

They Just Won't Listen

"Most people do not listen with the intent to understand;
they listen with the intent to reply."
—STEPHEN COVEY—

Before the start of every escape room the game master goes over all the rules of the game. These rules are shown on rather large posters at the entrance to every room. The Rules are as follows:

+ If you see a "do not touch sticker," that
  means it's not a part of the game.
+ No climbing. There is nothing in the ceiling.
+ Nothing needs pried open, unscrewed, or forced open.
+ Don't put anything in the outlets.
+ Nothing needs to be removed from the walls.
+ No pictures or videos.
+ Please use the restrooms before playing.
+ We can hear and see you at all times.
+ Please, only write on the dry erase boards.
+ You get three hints per game. Raise your hand or
  ask for a hint.
+ After you use a key to unlock something, you are
  done with that key for the rest of the game.

After you complete a clue or puzzle, you won't need to use it again for the rest of the game. The rule we place the most emphasis on is the three hints rule. At any point in the game, the players can all raise their hands and ask the game master to give them a hint. Typically, they would ask for some assistance when they reach a part where they are stuck and can't figure anything else out on their own. At that point, we will come over the microphone and lead them in the right direction. We stress this rule with the customers because all of our escape rooms are designed to be a level of difficulty that typically requires you use the three hints throughout the game. People can get out without using all three hints, but this is on extremely rare occasions. Most of the time, the groups use all three hints and still have the possibility to fail the game. No one has ever escaped using no hints.

Sometimes I tell a group that if I come over the microphone and ask them if they want a hint, it's a sign that the group members might need one. They don't have to take the suggestion, of course, and it can be used at the players' discretion. This happened to a group that played our Area D Nuclear room. It was the first escape game this family had ever played; so, it had no clue what to expect from the experience. Before the game began, I took extra time to go over the rules to ensure they understood everything. I got to the part explaining that the group had three free hints to use, and I explained how to use them. I stressed to the group that this was our hardest room, with a 10 percent escape rate, and that it would be best to consider using a hint around the 45-, 30-, and 15-minute marks to make sure the group was still on track. I also told the group that if I came over the microphone and asked if the group would like to use its hint, then it is probably an appropriate time to use it. I also stressed the point that these rooms were designed to use all three hints. I asked everyone if he or she understood, to which the group members shook their heads up and down and replied "yes." That advice to use a hint isn't given to every group but rather to the groups that are playing one of our harder rooms for their first experience. Sometimes, for groups that have never done this before, I will give free advice, such as telling a group there are two possible paths to take throughout the game, so the group members don't all get held up on one thing.

This group received all the advice offered above and was ready to play the game; so, I put the group members in the room. Fifteen minutes into the game, they were struggling badly and not making any progress in the room; so, I came over the microphone and asked them if they wanted to receive a hint. The hope was that the group members remembered what I said, in the hallway prior to the game, about taking a clue if I asked them about it. Everyone in the room unanimously said no and continued playing the game. This wasn't a big deal to me, as it is their option to take hints and use them as they please. My job as a game master is to ensure they have the best experience possible while also playing the game the way they want to play. The group remained in the room, making little-to-no progress. I occasionally guided the group along by providing players with small nudges in the right direction, but nothing too major. Before I knew it, the group had only 30 minutes left to play the game. In that room the players of the game need to be at a certain point at a certain time, or close to it, in order to have a chance of winning. This group was not close to that point; so, I decided to ask group members again if they wanted to use their first hint. It didn't take them long to decide together that they still didn't want a hint, and they played on. That was the last time I would ask them, as I didn't want to continue bugging them if they weren't looking for my help. Remember, my job is to maximize the individual's experience with my company. Sometimes people prefer that we help them along the way because they want to win regardless of how many hints they use, and sometimes groups don't want to use a hint at all, which almost guarantees a failed escape room experience.

I watched in silence, wishing this group would somehow start figuring things out so that it may, if anything, get close to finishing the game. With 10 minutes left in the game, and at a point that they could no longer pass, the group asked for some assistance. I came over the microphone and gave players a double hint, without them realizing that I had, to help speed things along. This aided the group to progress further in a quicker period of time. It was coming down to the wire. The group had two minutes left and asked for its second hint. I gave the group a double hint again, but at that point it didn't matter if I gave group members 10 hints; they were too far behind. A bright flash, followed by a loud explosion, encompassed the room. The nuclear bomb went off, and everyone was evaporated in seconds.

When the group members came out of the Nuclear room, they were upset that they lost. They claimed it was impossible to win. Some of them were shaking their heads in disappointment. I took them to the lobby to get their end-of-game picture. Afterwards, I tried to encourage them, by reminding everyone that they just came out of our hardest room. They also now had experience in an escape room, and the next time around they'd do a lot better. This didn't seem to have the uplifting effect on the group that I had envisioned. As they were leaving, one of the group members mumbled under her breath, "No one probably wins these." With that, the group walked out the front door.

What happened with this group? To me it was obvious. They just didn't listen. Before the game I explained everything to all players in detail and emphasized the fact that they were playing a room with only a 10 percent escape rate. I stressed that they needed to use all three hints to have a chance, and, most importantly, on the rare occasion I would come over the microphone and ask them if they wanted a hint, they should probably take it. Unfortunately, what happened in the game was the opposite. Twice in the game, at the strategic times I told them before the game, the 45- and 30-minute marks, I asked them if they wanted to use their first hint. Both times during the experience, the group turned down my request. On top of not using help when they got stuck, or when I asked them if they wanted to use a hint, they got their first bit of game master support with only 10 minutes left in the game. The request for my advice with two minutes didn't do much to help them win the game either, as it was too late.

If this were a group that had experience with escape games before, I wouldn't have taken the extra step to make sure the players knew what to expect with the hints. However, I knew this family had never done a room before and picked the hardest room we offer, so I went out of my way to stress everything players needed to know about the three hints. I was on their side and wanted them to win. This wasn't a competition between them and me in which they shouldn't trust me. We were all in this together, and in this case, I was the expert, the one with experience watching this room hundreds of times the one who knew where they should always be throughout the game. My title is game master, not game guesser. In my opinion, there were two reasons they didn't pass. One reason is that they wanted to beat the room themselves and didn't want help achieving that goal. The second reason, which has been the case most of the time with groups like this one, is that when the rules were shared, the group just didn't listen. Not listening at key moments in the game is one thing, but not listening at all throughout the process is another. The next group was the latter.

Punctuality from our customers is extremely important. The start time for every game at the Great Escape is already set in advance. On weekends, especially Saturdays, we typically sell out or get very close to it. Since our games run on a set schedule, if someone is late, it can throw off the entire night. For example, let's say the Bank Vault has games at 11:00 a.m., 12:15 p.m., 1:30 p.m., 2:45 p.m., and 4:00 p.m., and every time slot has players booked to play. If the group playing the 11:00 a.m. spot shows up 15 minutes late and fails the game (spends the entire hour playing), then the 12:15 p.m. will be delayed and possibly the 1:30 p.m., 2:45 p.m., and 4:00 p.m. We allow a five-minute grace period but have told people in the past that we can't start their game if they are very late, as it will have an impact on the game after theirs.

I was working one Saturday when a group of individuals came into Great Escape to book a game that they would play later in the night. They decided to go with the Prison Break because they had never played an escape game and that scenario offered the highest escape rate percentage. It was a Saturday; so, I stressed to them that they should arrive at 7:30 p.m. since their game started at 7:45 p.m. They agreed and left the building. I originally was the game master on Area D all night, but we had an empty time slot for that room around 7:30 p.m.; so, I switched rooms and decided to run the 7:45 p.m. Prison game.

I was at the front desk waiting for the group to show up when the clock struck 7:45 p.m. I called the number they'd left me, and a group member picked up. I told her I was calling from the Great Escape Game, that I noticed her group had a 7:45 p.m. game booked that night with us, and I wanted to make sure they didn't need any help with finding the place (knowing they had been there earlier in the day and knew where it was). She informed me that they were almost there and got off the phone with me. 7:50 p.m. came around, and they strolled into the lobby. I greeted them and confirmed that they were my 7:45 p.m. Prison Break group. We were already behind, but I asked if anyone needed to use the restroom, as we would be in the room for an hour. One of the individuals from the group took me up on my suggestion to use the lavatory. After another five minutes had passed, I took everyone to the Prison Break entrance.

I started going over the rules with the group members, when two more of them said they had to use the restroom. I reluctantly agreed, and the other group members and I waited for them to come back. At this point we were already 15 minutes past the time we should have started the game. I then realized that I only had two out of the six players with me waiting to go over the rules. I was already postponing for what seemed like forever for the two to come back from the restrooms. In the meantime, I was looking for the other two that had disappeared from the group. I located these two in the Tomb hallway taking selfies by one of the columns. I asked them to follow me to the Prison room and informed them that we were running behind and needed to get started. The woman started arguing with me and said it wasn't their fault that they were late. I didn't respond, but I was thinking to myself, "Whose fault was it then?" Finally, I had all six players and I started to go over the rules again. I noticed that not everyone in the group was paying attention; so, I had to go over a couple instructions again to make sure that items such as using hints and emergency information were heard.

Finally, 20 minutes after the time that we should have started, I got the group in the room and handcuffed everyone to the wall (the group members are in a jail after all). On the end of the handcuffs are magnets that attach to the wall. These magnets can easily be removed from the wall should an emergency happen. While handcuffing them, I reminded the group that players were to take the magnets, which hold the handcuffs to the wall, off only during an emergency. I started the game video and headed to the game master room. Within 30 seconds, one of the group members had removed the magnet from the wall and was roaming around. I got on the microphone and asked him to reattach the magnet to the wall, to which he complied. As you would imagine, the game moved at a very slow pace. I helped this group a little more than I would a normal group because I knew it was this group's first escape room experience.

The group got to a point in the game in which a player has to stick a broom down a sink to get a wrench that would help them sneak through a secret passageway. I convinced the group members to use a hint and told them they might need to stick the broom down something in the room to find an object that they were looking for. There is a magnet on the end of one of the brooms that grabs the wrench down the drain, and sometimes it takes a couple of tries to get the magnet to stick to the wrench. The players gave it a go, but the broom didn't grab the wrench the first try. They gave up on the sink and proclaimed that there was nothing down there even after I told them that there was. I got back on the microphone and told them they should try to stick the broom down the sink again to grab the wrench that was on the bottom of the drain. Someone told me that they had already tried that, and the group members continued to walk around the room not doing what I told them had needed to be done. They just didn't listen.

Luckily for them this was our easiest room with a pass rate above 50 percent, or else they wouldn't have made it that far in the game. With luck, and a lot of extra hints, the group eventually managed to get into the secret passageway and through to the final room of the prison. Inside the final room there is a container that needs to be opened. This container doesn't have a lock on it and is opened by an RFID card; although, the players in the rooms don't know that. One of the players, remembering the broom had a magnet on the bottom of it, grabbed the broom and began putting the base of the broom all over the box hoping that would open it. At the beginning of every room I tell the groups that once they use something to finish a puzzle in any of our tasks, they won't need to use it again. The broom in this case was no different. I came over the microphone and reminded these players that they were done with the broom and wouldn't need it again. That person set the broom down and almost immediately another person picked it up and tried the same thing on the box. I quickly came over the microphone yet again and told the players that they do not need the broom and that it will not be used another time for the remainder of the game. The player set the broom down. In the blink of an eye a third person picked up the broom to give it a try. Keep in mind there are speakers in every room allowing everyone to hear the game master—in this case, me—speak (all they have to do is listen); so, I know they all could hear me say that they were done with the broom. My voice boomed over the microphone, in a loud and clearly annoyed tone, telling them not to touch the broom again. The group chuckled a bit, took the broom back into the room where group members had found it, and continued playing the game. One of my employees was in the same game master room with me but watching a different game on a monitor next to me. He thought it was hilarious and was chuckling over the broom fiasco. Finally, the saga with the broom was over. All players now knew that they didn't have to use the broom anymore and that it wouldn't help them for the rest of the game. A minute went by, and then the unthinkable happened.

Remember that lady that went to the restroom before the game started and was found taking selfies in the Tomb hallway and then proceeded to tell me it wasn't her fault for being late? It was her, broom in hand, leaving the room where the broom should have remained, heading to the final room. Before the lady could even try to open the container with the broom, I came over the microphone in a very brash voice and stated, "Put the broom down!" I then repeated three times in a row "Please don't touch the broom again." My employee watching the game next to me was dying of laughter at this point. I've watched enough games to know when a group is being obnoxious on purpose and when players just don't get it. In this case the group wasn't getting it.

The group broke down and used a hint, which got the group members into the container. Inside this box was the second to last puzzle in the room. They were so close to victory. On the clue card it asked them to find four objects in the rooms they had already discovered, which would give them a numerical four-digit code. The group had less than two minutes left in the game and was running around frantically to find the objects on the clue card. They had gotten three of the four required numbers but had gotten one of the numbers wrong. I came over the microphone and told them the second number was incorrect. None of the players seemed to move after I told them this. I told them again that the second number needed correcting. Still no reaction. When I come over the microphone, I can hear my voice through the speakers, and I know they should be able to hear me. For the third and final time I loudly told them the second number was not right and should be a different number. It was too late. The warden and a gang of corrections officers busted through the prison doors. Time was up. Handcuffed again, the prisoners were escorted back to their cells. They were frustrated and asked what they did wrong. I stared at them with a dazed look on my face. Did they seriously just ask me that? I told them about the wrong number and asked if they could hear me over the microphone. They all replied, "Yes, we heard you." In disbelief, I walked them to the lobby, took their picture, and reset my room. From before the game began, during the game and through-out, there was only one problem that held them back every step of the way: they just didn't listen.

A few weeks later, a corporate party booked two games on a Monday afternoon. The organization had nine people and split up those individuals into two rooms: The Bank Vault and the Outbreak. None of the guests had played a room before; so, I told them one of the rooms would be the easiest room we offer, and the other room was the second hardest. One of the teams volunteered itself for the easier room, the Bank Vault, and I decided to be their game master. I went over the rules and brought them into the room. One of the first things that happens in our Bank Vault room is an alarm goes off. You start off the robbery in the dark and within a couple minutes you will find a key that opens a box with a lever that illuminates the room. Once you hit the lights, the alarm sounds and doesn't turn off until you figure out the password, which is entered on the digital keypad. The alarm is usually shut off within the first 10 minutes of the game.

Fifteen minutes had gone by in the Bank Vault, and the alarm was still sounding. Directly underneath the alarm are four sets of keys labeled security alarm keys. Each set has a different number of keys. To shut off the alarm, one must count the number of keys in each set, which gives you the code to turn the annoying beeping sound off. I came over the microphone and told the group it needed to count the security keys to shut off the alarm. Instead of looking at the security alarm keys and counting them, the players went over to a box on a wall that had keys in it. I told them they were in the wrong spot and that they needed to look at the security alarm keys directly under the alarm. One of the players told me that there were keys inside the box on the wall. This was true, but these were not the keys they needed yet. After some persuasion, the players found the security alarm keys and turned off the alarm.

Within each game there are certain points that teams need to reach to be on track to win or at least to come close to it. The group was already behind; so, I came over the microphone to give the players some free advice. I asked them if they had opened the blue moneybag in the room. This moneybag can be found in the unlocked bottom right desk drawer. Sometimes the game master can't see where the money bag is because the players can set the bag down on a table and then stand in front of it, obscuring it's view from the camera. However, in this case, they hadn't found the moneybag yet. I told them to check the unlocked bottom right drawer on the desk. One of the ladies, quick to reply, stated that she already checked that drawer. After hearing her response, the players stopped checking the desk and continued playing the game. I told them again to check the unlocked bottom right desk drawer. Upon hearing my advice, one of the players opened the top middle drawer on the desk and searched inside the drawer thoroughly. "Third time is a charm," I thought to myself. "Open the bottom right desk drawer," I said. Finally, after a painful two minutes, they opened the unlocked bottom right desk drawer containing the blue moneybag.

A couple of minutes later, the players found a key that gave them access to a locker on the wall of one of the "bank employees." Inside this locker they find a grabby tool and some cash. Across the room from the locker there is a box on the wall with a transparent glass front that you can see through, as well as three holes in the side of the box. Inside this box are three keys hanging on the wall. Players use the grabby tool to fish the keys out through the holes in the sides of the box. Upon discovering the grabby tool, the players walked around the room with it. After about 30 seconds they gave up on the grabby tool and then set it down on top of the box that they needed to use the tool on. I waited a couple of minutes for them to come back to the grabby tool, but they didn't. I came across the microphone and told them they would need to use the grabby tool to fish the keys out of the box on the wall. They picked up the tool from the box and brought it across the room to the lockers and tried to unlock the lockers with the tool. Once again, I came over the microphone to clarify that they needed to use the tool on the box on the wall where the keys can be seen. I heard one of the girls in the group say, "Oh ok," and grab the tool from the guy. Instead of walking across the room to use the tool on the box I told them to use it on, she tried to unlock a different locker on the wall. I had to come over the microphone and tell the girl to stop, turn around, and walk to the other side of the room. Luckily for my sanity, she gave up on the locker, found the box on the wall, and started fishing for the keys.

There are four employee lockers on the wall in the Bank Vault. At this point in the game three of the four employee lockers have been opened. The third locker in the locker row remains closed, and the key to that locker can be found hidden inside the second locker towards the top. Almost all groups fail to find the hidden key in the second employee locker, even though it's in plain sight. This assembly of individuals was no different and was struggling badly in the room. I came over the microphone and asked the players if they would like to use a hint, and they all agreed. I told them they might want to double-check the open employee lockers on the wall. Almost immediately, one of individuals told me they had already checked the lockers. Fortunately, a couple of the players still went over to investigate but came up empty-handed. I came over the microphone again to tell them to search the top of the lockers. When giving hints to a group, you never want to tell players directly how to accomplish something. It's always more fun for the players when they feel like they solved the problem themselves. A couple of the players looked through the lockers again and proclaimed that there was nothing inside of them. Enough with the subtleties! I came over the microphone and told them there was a hidden key attached to the top of the second employee locker. "No there isn't!" replied one of the players. This player was certain that there wasn't a key there. As a game master, I'm not trying to deceive anyone. My goal is to aid when someone needs help. After pleading with the players to look on top of the second locker, someone finally discovered the key, and game play continued. Don't get me wrong, I don't expect anyone to go into a room he or she has never been inside before, play a game he or she has never played, and have all the answers. In fact, I'm terrible at playing escape rooms. My success in previous escape rooms was due to the abilities of the players in the rooms with me. However, when a game master comes over the microphone to help you and tells you to do a specific action, then it's best if you focus on what they are suggesting.

On each desk in the game master room there is a card that lets you know where a team needs to be time-wise in a game. This group was very far behind, and unless I didn't help the players considerably, they would flop badly. Earlier in the game a black light is found in one of the lockers. Players need to find a small symbol in the room on an HVAC vent by using the black light. Later in the game another object comes up with the same symbol on it painted with black light paint. At that point, both symbols are matched together, and a secret compartment will open. The group was at the point where it had discovered the object with the symbol on it and needed to find the corresponding character in the room to match it up with. I told the players that it was required for them to find the same symbol in the room and told them which corner it was in. They were using the black light on the wall and weren't finding it, so I told them to look lower with the light. Pretty straightforward, right? All they had to do was flash the light lower than where they were looking. What happened next shouldn't have surprised me. The player using the black light started going up with the light. "No, look lower," I said, but higher and higher he went until he was looking at the ceiling with the light. I thought I was losing my mind. There was another game master in the room with me when this was going on, and he came over to watch my game with me. He couldn't believe it either. Third time was usually a charm with this group; so, I spoke slowly and clearly and told group members to put the light on a very specific spot in the room where the matching symbol is. This worked, and they successfully opened the secret HVAC safe. After opening the RFID compartment, the players needed to move quickly. They only had five minutes left in the game and were past the point of being able to escape the room. I at least wanted to get them to the puzzle that would produce the code to the safe. That way I could say they were almost there without having to lie to them. If I could get them through one more puzzle, they would be at a point that was close enough to victory.

Throughout the game the players find pieces to a security map that has many camera systems on it as well as the directions to the Vault. Reading the directions to the Vault, players will have to locate a series of camera systems that have numbers on them on the map that they have assembled. The numbers on the camera systems form the code needed to unlock the security box. There are eight digits in total. Since the game was going to be over soon, I informed the group that it would need eight numbers. Four numbers would be found from the left side of the map on the first floor and four numbers from the right side of the map, which corresponds to the second floor. The players seemed to have understood me and started looking at the map. The numbers they get from this are entered on a camera security box that is on the desk in the room. On this security box is a large label that says, "Ask before entering code," as well as a statement that says, "Three or more wrong entries, and the safe will lock out permanently." Each time a player enters a number on the security box it makes a loud beep. The players knew they needed eight numbers, and they also knew where they would need to enter these numbers once they got them. After a minute of looking at the map, one of the players walked over to the security box and started typing in the code. Beep, beep, beep. Three beeps are all I heard. Three beeps meant that only three numbers were entered in the safe. I came over the microphone and told them they are looking for eight numbers and reminded them to ask me before entering the code into the security box.

Without hesitation, the person started entering more numbers in the safe. I came over the sound system again and told him one more wrong entry would lock the safe out for good. Much to my relief the guy walked away from the security box. There was only one-minute left in the game. I asked them what eight numbers they had gotten from the map. They read off six numbers and asked if that was correct. "You need eight numbers," I proclaimed, to which they almost collectively replied, "We need eight numbers?" With that, their time had expired, and the cops had come to place them all under arrest. At that point I was ready, willing, and able to handcuff them myself and throw them in the back of the cop car.

The worst part wasn't the fact that they were bad at the escape room but rather their lack of communication skills. I got a chance to talk to them a little after their game and discovered the players in the room were in their thirties and worked at a local hospital. Think about that next time you pay your local clinic a visit. Sure, they didn't do well in the room, but the reason for their failure wasn't a result of their lack of escape room experience. Their catastrophe was due to a problem that was as plain as day: they just didn't listen. This group was frustrating to watch. However, there are times when groups that don't listen in the Bank Vault can be entertaining—at least for me.

The Bank Vault is one of my favorite rooms to watch. This room is our second easiest out of the six we offer, boasting around a 50 percent escape rate. It's our most straight-forward room regarding the difficulty level of the puzzles and clues as well as the looks inside the room. The main theme with the Bank Vault is trickery and hidden objects. As one would expect, there are a lot of keys in the Bank Vault experience. All of the keys, expect one, are hidden somewhere in the room. Most of them are hidden but accessible in the first 10 minutes, but rarely do players find any of them in this 10-minute time period. The reason this room is my favorite is because the hint I give is always the same. The hint is "Are you sure you checked?" and then I tell the group whatever the object is that they hasn't discovered yet. This can happen up to seven times in the Bank Vault, in which I must ask the players if they are sure they checked something to which they have access. Every progressive time throughout the game that I must ask that question, I get more animated and drag out the question, which sounds more like this: "Are you surrrrrrrrre you checked that?" Asking that question gets more fun for me—and sometimes for the group—each time they don't find something and need my help.

Occasionally, we'll have a group that isn't as entertained as I am when it can't find the hidden keys and must hear the same relenting question from me. I remember one group that couldn't find the first key in the game. I gave the players about five minutes before coming over the microphone to pop the question (the question being a hint, not a marriage proposal). I got them with the first "Are you sure?" and object reveal, and someone in the group swore up and down that the group had checked that spot already. A couple of minutes later the group asked for a hint. I hit the group members with another "Are you sure you checked?" question for a different hidden object, and a different group member stated that she already looked there. The group found the next key, but you could sense a little frustration. My favorite hidden key can be found from the start of the game but is usually found around the 10-minute mark. This key is right in front you, and 99 percent of the time no one finds it. The group was stuck and asked for its second hint. I came over the microphone in a tone that to players probably sounded like a nagging parent and asked the dreaded question, "Are you sure you checked this particular object?" A guy in the group said, "Yes, I already checked that. There is nothing there." The group members listened to their teammate and didn't even attempt to look at the spot where I had directed them. I asked again if they were sure they checked this spot in the room. The response from the group was unanimous: yes, they had already looked, and there was nothing there. They were convinced of it. This was the third time in the game I hit them with the "Are you sure you checked this?" question that always led to a hidden key or object. If you are reading this and haven't played the game yourself, you might be thinking the hidden keys are too hard to find but I assure you they aren't. The last key in question has a magnet on it and is on top of the inside of the second locker on the wall. If you look up in there, you can see it.

As a game master, I wasn't there to lie to or trick them, and I knew they didn't have the key. This time I changed my approach, and instead of hitting them with an "Are you sure?" I told them to double check this item in the room. With a raised voice, a guy in the room proclaimed there was nothing in there. At this point, someone else in the group started to search in the area and found the key. They were almost upset when they found it. The key was right in front of them the entire time. One would think that after the third time of me asking if they'd double-checked something, they would go back to it if I asked them again. Such was not the case. Toward the end of the game, there is a code that is hidden in plain sight. It's one of the last things players need to accomplish in the game before collecting all the loot and escaping. This group was down to its last hint. With two minutes left in the game, the sirens came on, and it was do-or-die time. I came over the microphone and asked the question, "Are you sure you checked the...?" The group responded almost as one cohesive unit and said yes. I asked again because the group was nearly out of time. "Yes, we already checked that, and there is nothing there!" Boom, times up! Everyone was under arrest. The code to the small safe in front of the players was written with black light marker and was written on the safe itself. The group members were upset that they didn't pass the room and refused to get their picture taken. As they were leaving, I could hear them mutter how this room was impossible. It was disappointing to hear them say this because they were only one minute away from victory. However, and more importantly, it wasn't that the room was impossible; it was the fact that they just didn't listen.

OBSERVATION 6

Put distractions aside,
and take the time to truly listen to someone.

CHAPTER SEVEN

We Just Don't Listen

"Most of the successful people
I've known are the ones who do more
listening than talking."
—BERNARD BARUCH—

I was with my business partner one night discussing marketing ideas, when an email popped up on my phone. It was a one-star Google review from a customer. I take all my reviews very seriously; so, when I received that notification I was extremely concerned. My mission with the Great Escape Game is to do my best to ensure my customers have the most rewarding experience possible. The reason the business exists is to help individuals escape reality in a fun way. In the review the customer claimed that the game master was not paying attention to her group and didn't listen to the group members' several requests for hints and assistance. She mentioned she would never go to our establishment again. I showed my business partner the email, and we immediately headed up to the Great Escape to review the video and audio of the room in question. The customers played Area D, and my business partner and I watched the game from start to finish.

I didn't know what to expect when I started watching the tape. We have a ton of reviews, and it is extremely rare for the Great Escape Game to get a bad one.

I was expecting to watch the game and see one opportunity that the game master missed to engage with the customer in the room, resulting in the poor review; I was way off in my assumption. In the first two minutes of the game one of the players asked the game master a question. I waited to hear a response, but it didn't come. Seven minutes later, a lady in the room asked how many times she could enter a code into a security box. She received no reply to her inquiry. Twelve minutes later, one of the guys in the room mentioned something about a hint. It was faint, and no one raised their hand suggesting they wanted one, which wasn't a big deal. Then, the worst-case scenario happened. Twenty-seven minutes into the game all five players in Area D raised their hands and asked for a hint. Their hands seemed to stay in the air for an eternity. It was hard for me to watch. There was a sickness in my stomach. I sat there in silence and waited and waited and waited. Nothing happened. After 15 long seconds, the customers realized they weren't getting any support and put their hands down. No hint was ever given. I had to pause the game after that moment to sit and think for a couple of minutes. I felt like I failed as a business owner and as a manager. I let my employees down by not providing them with enough training, and I also let the five individuals playing Area D down by ruining their experience in one of my escape rooms.

My job reviewing the tape wasn't over though, and I hit play to resume watching. Five minutes later, one of the players asked a question about the keyboard in the room and got no response. More than halfway through the game, the unthinkable happened. The players in the room raised their hands again, looking for a hint. At this point I was so embarrassed I couldn't even watch the screen while their hands were in the air. I simply closed my eyes and sat there waiting to hear anything from the game master who was running the room. I felt helpless and was begging to hear the voice that would provide the players with assistance. Once again, silence was the only thing coming through the speakers, and it was louder than any noise I have heard before. At this point in the game the customers had audibly complained six times about the game master not listening.

A couple of minutes later one of the guys in the room asked another question out loud, and finally the game master answered. For the next 15 minutes the game master responded to any questions asked by the players. With five minutes left the players asked for help again, and the game master came over the microphone and talked about something they had accomplished 15 minutes prior. During the last three minutes of play, one of the ladies in the room was talking loudly about the fact that the game master wasn't paying attention to the game. She was right in her assertion that we just didn't listen.

The next day, I contacted that customer first thing in the morning and refunded her money, as well as provided her with a free room on us. I apologized and promised her group's experience next time would be a great one. I asked the game master to come in the next day and made him watch the entire game. It was the last time anyone at the Great Escape would not pay attention to a game. My game master and I had dropped the ball, but he was quick to apologize and has been stellar ever since. I wasn't upset with the game master. We all make mistakes, and hopefully we learn from them. There have been plenty of times throughout my life and career at Great Escape that I didn't listen when I should have. It's so easy to point out when others don't listen to us, yet sometimes it's us that don't do a decent job listening ourselves. Understanding when we do that and taking action to listen more will make our lives and the lives of others around us better.

OBSERVATION 7

Being a good listener is hard work,
but it's worth every effort.

CHAPTER EIGHT

Learn, Evolve, and Adapt

"The key to success
is often the ability to adapt."
—ANTHONY BRANDT—

Building an escape room was one of the most exciting parts of owning this business. It all begins with discovering what the theme of the room will be. There are seemingly endless room themes to pick from, all with their pros and cons. One of the first themes we came up with was a submarine room. Players would be trapped in a sinking sub and would have one hour to find the escape pod and a way to navigate to the surface before being crushed by the weight of the water above. Our plan was to have pipes hanging from a low ceiling and at one point we thought about filling the room with water to make it as realistic as possible. Unfortunately, building the submarine room seemed too difficult at the time and we had come up with another game that we felt would appeal to a wider range of customers. We decided on building a Bank Vault-themed room. After all, who doesn't want to rob a bank?

The room design for the Bank Vault was accomplished inside one of the bedrooms in my house. Inside that bedroom, I had painted dry erase paint on all four walls earlier in the month. This room served as my idea space where I would write down business ideas on the walls. Once we discovered that we were going to pursue an escape game business and that we wanted to build a bank for our first room, we erased all the business ideas and started designing our very first room, the Bank Vault. We were so excited about building the Bank Vault that we stayed up all night drawing it out. We didn't sleep that night, and after almost 20 straight hours we had already built the layout and game ideas for the room. We determined quickly how everything was going to be laid out as well as where keys and puzzles were to be hidden. However, knowing where everything was made us feel like each room was entirely too easy, which made planning the timing of the room very difficult. For example, one of the keys to a locker can be found under the security guard's desk. For us finding this key should only take a minute or two when in reality it took ten minutes of longer most of the time.

My business partner had told me that the puzzles weren't hard enough in the rooms and that everyone was going to fly through them—and for a second, I started to believe him, but we were about to learn the hard way on opening weekend that the rooms weren't as easy as we originally thought. Opening day was on a Saturday. We didn't have many expectations on being busy, as we had spent zero dollars in advertising leading up to our grand opening but ended up booking out 11 time slots for the day. It was a great first day and gave us good energy from the get-go. The only problem with day one was that everyone that played an escape room that day had failed—and failed badly. Our two rooms, the Outbreak and the Bank Vault, were not only difficult but also impossible. Puzzles and clues in the room that we thought would be easy to accomplish turned out to be nearly unsolvable. I specifically remember one clue card in the Outbreak game that required players to look on the clue card for four words, locate those words at various places in the room, and then get a code from them. They would use these four words in conjunction with a poster on the wall that had the same four words. The four words were hidden in the clue card, which had paragraphs of information with no indication that these particular words were important. After several groups failed to discover the four words on their own, we wrote the four words in red font on the clue card to make matching the words and the poster easier. Looking back, we can only laugh at how hard that puzzle was.

Getting customer feedback was so important to us, especially with the first dozen or so groups to play. After every game, we went through the rooms with the groups and indirectly asked their opinions on as many puzzles as we could. When customers raved or mentioned that they thought a part of a game was fun, or challenging in a clever way, we'd keep that puzzle, and sometimes we would even look to improve on it. However, there were a couple of puzzles and clues that the customers would consistently say they didn't like or that they thought to be annoying. Even if this puzzle, clue, or part of the game had been something we loved, if the customers didn't want it in there, we would adjust accordingly. Over a period of several months, our rooms became the types of rooms that we had envisioned from the start. It's been months since I've heard a customer complain about something in any of our rooms. Listening to customers can sometimes work wonders. Not listening could have spelled disaster for us.

OBSERVATION 8

Always be learning and adapting.

CHAPTER NINE

The First Date

*"I hate first dates. I made the mistake of telling my date
a lie about myself, and she caught me. I didn't think
she'd actually demand to see the bat cave."*

−ALEX REED−

I think it's safe to assume that all of us have gone on a bad, or at least an uninteresting date, at some point in our lives. Some of us have gone on so many dates we could probably write a book on those experiences. Date nights are an extremely common occurrence at the Great Escape Game. After all, who wouldn't want to be locked in a room for an hour in an extremely stressful environment with their significant other (yeah, that was sarcasm)? I've pretty much seen it all when it comes to couples playing a room. From couples yelling at each other, threatening to break up, to the ones that communicate with each other so well you'd think their life depended on it.

My favorite story involving two (almost) lovebirds happened on a rainy summer day in 2016. Our business can pick up dramatically if the weather outside is poor. When it's beautiful and sunny, there are a ton of different options of things to do besides play an escape game, and we can find ourselves less busy. When it rains or when it starts to get cold is when we see our bookings increase substantially. I was at the front desk one Wednesday afternoon when I got a call from a nervous-sounding man. He said he was supposed to go on a first date tonight with a girl he met on Tinder. He was planning to take her to a Dayton Dragons game, which is the local single-A minor league baseball team. It was supposed to rain that night, and he was calling about availability on our rooms just in case the game got called off. He asked me over the phone if I thought an escape game was a good idea for a first date. "Absolutely" I said without hesitation. After all, as a business owner, what was I supposed to say?

Now, some might argue that being locked in a room with a stranger wouldn't be one of their top ten things to do on a first date list; nonetheless, I persuaded him that it would be a stellar idea to bring her. It ended up raining that day, and the guy called again to book an escape room. I talked him into the Bank Vault because it's the best room to be able to pass with just two people. Their game was scheduled for 7:30 p.m. and they both arrived on time. I'm an optimist and thought to myself, "Hey, what could go wrong here?" It didn't take long for me to start doubting myself after I saw the guy finish off the orange energy drink that was in his hand. What's wrong with having an energy drink before an escape game? There's nothing wrong with having one energy drink before playing a game per se. The problem with this guy was that after he finished off his first energy drink, he pulled another one out of his pocket and opened it. He asked if he could bring the beverage into the room, and I told him that he was not allowed to.

I performed my obligatory pregame speech and asked them if they needed to use the restroom before the game. They both informed me that they didn't have to go to the lavatory: so, it was time to begin. I was ready to put them in the room—when the guy told me to hold on, took his second energy drink, and chugged the entire thing. That's right, he had at least one-and-a-half energy drinks before being locked in a room with a girl he'd never met before on a first date. I'm not talking about a small drink either; it was one of those monstrous cans that should take someone all day to finish. I've never had an energy drink before and don't know personally how long they take to kick in, but the effects on this guy seemed to happen right away. I was going over the rules, and he couldn't focus at all. His lack of attention was so bad that I asked him if he understood what the objective of the game was and if he had any questions. While he was standing there shaking, he nodded at me, informing me with his gestures that he was good, and with that I put them in the room.

The best part of the Bank Vault is that the game starts with the lights off, and the switch to turn them on is locked, which, in this case, added to the excitement (for me and him that is). As I mentioned in a previous chapter, after the players get the lights on, an alarm is tripped in the Bank Vault. This constant beeping and strobing of the alarm light continues until the players shut it off by entering a code into the alarm itself. Players have unlimited guesses to try to shut off the alarm. There are a ton of distractions and numbers in the room that could be the code to shut off the alarm, but there's only one code that works. This guy shifted into third gear, ran around the room frantically looking for numbers, and then ran back to the alarm to try them out. He never tried to communicate with the girl in the room or offer to work together to solve the alarm or even let her put in a potential combination. At one point he ran into her while trying to hurry back to the alarm to try out a combination. I couldn't take it anymore and came over the microphone to give them a free hint to help turn off the alarm.

After the alarm was disabled, the guy continued being frantic in the room. At one point he went to the trash can in the room, turned it upside down, picked it up over his head and started shaking it. He then threw the trashcan down and continued his path of destruction. The poor helpless woman tried to communicate with him, but on every occasion, it didn't work out in her favor. In the middle of the game the woman found a clue and told him that she found something. He rushed over to her, grabbed it out of her hands, and hurried around the room trying to make sense of it. She just stood there in disbelief as we both watched the show go on. The rest of the time went on in this same disorganized manner. The final minute was upon them, and it was obvious that they would not be winning the game. This was unacceptable to the guy, as he proceeded to go over to the big safe in the room and tried to force the door open while screaming at the top of his lungs in an apparent rage. The game was finally over, and I brought them out of the room to the lobby. To my surprise (more sarcasm), the girl didn't want to get an end of game picture. It was as plain as day that she was completely over it and wanted to escape out of there as fast as she could. He then asked her if she wanted to go to the bar next door to grab a drink. She claimed she had to get going, thanked him for the escape room, and left the building. Words of wisdom for all you guys out there trying to woo a girl on a first date, lay off the energy drinks. Be cool, calm, and collected. If you are relaxed, she is relaxed.

OBSERVATION 9

Always be cool, calm, and collected.

CHAPTER TEN

Does Age Make a Difference?

"Sometimes age succeeds; sometimes it fails. It depends on you."
—RAVENSARA NOITE—

One of the most interesting things I've observed in escape rooms is the difference in behavior between older and younger crowds. Our games are designed for players aged 13 years and older. We don't often get super young kids who want to play. On the opposite end of the spectrum, our escape rooms don't have an age limit so to speak, but we usually don't have too many people over the age of 65 come through. So, for sake of this chapter I will be talking about the behavior I've observed from individuals between the ages of 13 to 65. Although the following scenarios are individual games, the observations and patterns of these descriptions occur in most of the related age groups. We'll dive right into the differences between youth and experience with a couple of stories from our Outbreak room, followed by the Bank Vault.

A group of individuals in their 50s was attempting to escape our Outbreak room. This scenario is our second hardest room; so, any mistakes made could be costly. Inside the Outbreak experience there are two rooms. The door leading into the second room is locked with an electronic keypad on it. Players usually get the code for the door and are in the second room within 15 minutes of the start of the game. Inside the first room there is a bottle game that, when solved, provides the code to the door to the other room. This puzzle is very tricky and takes most groups awhile to figure out. In addition to the keypad on the door, there is also a four-digit padlock attached to a different puzzle on the other side of the same room. Most players think when they get the four-digit code from the bottle game that it goes to the padlock and not the door; so, they try the lock first. This group was no different, and, after receiving the four-digit code, its players spent a minute trying to open the lock instead of the door.

While teammates were attempting to open the lock, an older woman in the group looked at the door, pondering whether to try it. I could see her brain telling her that the code might work on the door. She looked at it for a couple of seconds, took a step toward the door, and then shook her head and walked away. She was right! All she had to do was to take another step forward and input the code in the door, and it would have unlocked. The woman continued to walk around the room looking for clues to the game. At that moment, a man from the group walked up to the door, put his finger on the keypad, stopped for just a second, and decided not to try the code in the door! Two people in a single group had the right idea but didn't follow through with giving it a try.

Five minutes went by before someone inputted the code into the door and gained access to the second room. The group ended up not passing the room and only would've needed about five more minutes to win. What happened? Both individuals had the right code, and all they needed to do was input it into the door. There was no punishment or repercussion if the code didn't work, and, therefore, they had nothing to lose by trying it. However, they hesitated. Something in their minds told them that they shouldn't try it. Maybe it was a fear of being wrong or looking silly in front of the group. Maybe they needed more assurance that their choice made sense. Either way, they didn't attempt inputting the code into the door, and it cost them the game.

In an overwhelming majority of the hundreds of Outbreak games I've watched, there is one constant. The older the individuals are in the group, the less likely they are to try the four-digit code on the door in a timely manner. In the same Outbreak room if a group of 13-year-old kids were in the room, and they obtained the four-digit code for the door, almost always one of the group members will walk up to the door and try it. There is never any hesitation inputting the code. Once they have a code and know it goes somewhere, they will try every possibility they can find. Even if they don't have the code, younger groups are inputting random numbers into the door. I've never once seen a younger person look at the door, think about putting in a code, second-guess him or herself, and then walk away. Never. They always give it a try or, at minimum, tell someone to.

So then, being younger helps win escape games, right? Not so fast. The dynamic of what I call the "door dilemma" gets more interesting when looking at the game the players must finish to get the door code in the first place. In this game players find a plastic box with two holes towards the top of the box, four holes below that, and two holes towards the bottom for a total of eight holes. Next to this plastic box are eight bottles and a clue card. These bottles are numbered one through eight, and the clue card tells players to arrange the bottles in a way two consecutive numbers do not touch. In other words, if the bottle numbered four is placed in the top right hole, then bottles numbered three and five couldn't be touching it in the adjacent spaces. It's a somewhat simple game, but it does take patience and a little bit of critical thinking to solve.

Who has the upper hand in this game: the older crowd with the hesitation to try the door or the younger crowd that will give it a go without any fear of consequences? As it relates to this specific game, the older crowd does a lot better most of the time. Why is that? The bottle game can be very frustrating at times. Right when a player thinks he or she has the right answer, someone else notices that some bottles are touching that shouldn't be, and the game must start all over. The younger generation will start trying to figure out the correct combination quickly, but if one player doesn't get it quickly enough, he or she will get distracted, or sometimes easily discouraged, and pass the game off to the next person to try it. This does not bode well for the team's ability to move past that game quickly because the second person often is starting from scratch and didn't learn anything from the previous individual. I've watched games in which multiple kids will try it and give up shortly after attempting to figure it out, wasting precious time. The older groups, when they know what the problem is and understand what task needs to be done, will show significantly more patience than the younger groups. Often one adult will start the bottle game and will stay on it until it is finished. When the task is known, adult players have no problem sticking to it. Patience, in this case at least, is a virtue for the older individuals, and not for the younger.

Let's shift our focus now from the Outbreak to the Bank Vault. This room offers its own challenges and opportunities for the younger and older crowds. Out of the six rooms we offer, the Bank Vault is the most straightforward. The experience isn't that complicated because the focus of the room is hidden objects and things that are right in front of the players the entire game, even when they don't notice. All of the other escape room experiences have puzzles and clues that can get rather complicated or have many parts to them. From the first mission in the Bank Vault to the last, what is needed is always right in front of the players. While I certainly don't want to give away all the tricks in the room, there are a couple of puzzles that get accomplished differently depending on the age of the participants. The first of these would be any of the initial hidden keys in the room at the start of the game. Some of the keys are right in front of the players. Without a doubt the young adults around the age of 13 are best with finding hidden keys. The younger crowd will open everything, take out drawers from the cabinets (even if they aren't supposed to), triple-search objects, and not have any hesitation with trying something. The younger players are far more curious, in general, than the older players. They usually don't hold back when they want to try something, especially when they have a group of similar-aged kids to encourage them. However, I have observed that if a younger person is with older adults, he or she tends to be milder and more reserved.

At the end of the Bank Vault experience, players obtain the combination of four numbers that gets them into the big safe located within the room. The big safe is a turn dial, and it takes a series of different passes in different directions to open. The instructions of how to open it are on the front of the safe. Opening the vault could probably be done easily the first try, assuming there were no distractions. However, by the time the players reach the safe, they typically have less than five minutes left in the game. Toward the end of the game, the video in the room that shows the timer starts getting louder, and police sirens can be heard from the speakers. This increases the stress of the situation and also impacts how the different types of groups react to it.

Let's pretend I had two Bank Vault rooms that were running simultaneously: one room with a group of younger individuals and the other room with a group of older individuals. Let's also pretend that both groups had two minutes left in the game, and each had obtained the safe combination at the exact same time. If I had to place money on which of these two groups would open the safe first, I would put my money on the older group every time. Keep in mind when I say younger group, I am referring to groups of kids that are around the age of 13. You might be thinking that the older group has more success because of their experiences. Perhaps they would have opened more of these types of safes in their lives, and you may be right in the assumption.

However, when I closely observe the two groups, I notice two main things that make the older crowd winners in the battle of safe opening. Older crowds tend to have traits of patience and the ability to block out distraction.

The first trait, patience, is the easiest to observe. There is a certain calm about an older person trying to open a safe. Almost always older players' actions are precise and meticulous. They understand the task at hand and show a level of attention that is unmatched in any of our other rooms. With laser focus they listen to the directions and slowly turn the dial until they have all the combinations inputted, opening the safe with relative ease. The younger generation's players may turn the dial more quickly and seem to have a jump-start on opening it, but their strength in speed is also their weakness. A move of the dial one or two clicks past where it needs to be, and the entire process must be started again. This overturning of the dial from younger individuals is common, but their failure is not due to the speed itself. There is something else that enters the equation that, in my opinion, is one of the biggest causes of them losing this battle of opening the safe more quickly than the older individuals. Failure in opening the safe, especially on the first try, for younger players, is the inability to block out distractions. The older group has years of practice focusing and aren't as affected by the disturbances that are going on around them. When a kid tries to open the safe, there are usually other kids around distracting the safe opener. This could be in the form of other players making noises, talking over each other while trying to give instructions on how to open the safe, or tapping on the safe opener's shoulder to remind them that they only have two minutes left in the game, right in the middle of their attempt. Both older and younger crowds have their unique strengths and weaknesses. It's important to try to understand one's abilities as well as what areas one needs to improve on in order to try to avoid falling into a stereotype.

OBSERVATION 10

Be patient yet curious!
Give it a go. There is no failure, only learning.

CHAPTER ELEVEN

Let Go of Your Pride

*"Pride is the parent of destruction; pride eats the
mind and the heart and the soul alive."*

−ANNE RICE−

On rare occasion, we have a group come in that walks on water (or at least it thinks it does). This group might boast that they are six out of six when it comes to winning escape rooms or it might be a first-time group that, in an arrogant tone, states that it will easily set the record. Whichever form it takes, there is one thing that most of these groups have in common, and that is stubbornness. When we put people in the room, we stress the importance of using their three hints. As I've mentioned in previous chapters, the experiences are designed to be extremely difficult and almost impossible to accomplish without using at least one hint. I had one group come in to play the Outbreak and while talking with the group members in the lobby, I discovered that they were six for six in completing rooms as a group. They had played all of the rooms at my local competitor's escape room business and were ready to give ours a shot. I explained that our rooms are harder than my competitor's six rooms and that this room, the Outbreak, was, at the time, our hardest room. When going over the rules I stressed the importance of using hints and reminded them that this room would be the hardest room they would have played to date. One of the women in the group told me, "We won't need any hints," and everyone else shook their heads in agreement.

I put the group members in the room, started the video for their scenario, and it was game on. They started off extremely well, solving puzzles at an above normal pace, until they arrived at their first major hurdle. The players spent the next several minutes looking around the room for the next clue without realizing what they were searching for was right in front of them the entire time. Five minutes went by and they were still stuck on that one puzzle. I came over the microphone and asked them if they wanted to use a hint. They all said "no" in unison and continued playing the game. A couple more minutes went by and the group figured out what to do and was progressing through the game once again. The next couple of puzzles were easy to figure out for the group, but moments later the players found themselves stuck again. For seven minutes, the individuals in the Outbreak wandered back and forth through the rooms not making any progress. This time they broke down and raised their hands in the air asking for a hint. I gave them the hint, and they were quickly on the ball again, solving that riddle with relative ease. With two minutes left the group was on the final part of the last puzzle in the Outbreak.

This is one of the hardest puzzles in any of our six rooms. They were running out of time and weren't making any progress on the game. They still had one hint left, which would save them from the deadly virus; so I came over the microphone and asked them if they wanted to use their last clue. To my surprise they said "no." I asked them if they were sure, and they said "yes." One would think that maybe they didn't know how much time was left in the game, but only seconds before, someone had looked at the TV and yelled out that they had two-and-a-half minutes left. I wanted them to win and watching them struggle without taking their last hint started making me nervous. I watched with anticipation, and anxiety, for the next two minutes as the group struggled with the final puzzle. I kept looking back and forth at the group and the time for what seemed like longer than the two minutes it had left. Finally, with 15 seconds left in the game the players asked for the final clue. At that point it was too late. The clock on the timer then struck zero, everyone's skin boiled, and they collapsed as the poison did its work. They had all "died from a deadly virus." Putting an end to the pretend scenario, I opened the door and explained how the final puzzle worked that the group was working on. It all made sense to them after I explained it. I tried to get their pictures taken after the game, but they were too upset and practically ran out of the building.

They couldn't believe they had failed, and, in all honestly, neither could I. Granted, they did use two of their three hints, but by not using their hints when they knew they were stuck or when I asked if they wanted to use one, it cost them the game. With two minutes left, not making any progress and knowing they were stuck, they should have said yes to me when I asked if they wanted to use their final hint. In the end, it was their stubbornness that caused them to lose the game. A team of great players that could have easily set a record in the room ended up failing because of its players' pride.

OBSERVATION 11

Let go of your pride, and admit when you need help.

CHAPTER TWELVE

Drunk, High, and Hopeless

"Alcohol may be man's worst enemy, but the Bible says love your enemy."
—FRANK SINATRA—

The Great Escape Game is located in Beavercreek, a suburb of Dayton, Ohio. The store is in a strip mall and is conveniently located five minutes off a major highway and five minutes away from a major United States Air Force Base. The location is great for my business partner and me because we live very close to our business. Four doors down from our escape room is a very popular bar called King's Table. Often, we have big corporate parties play escape rooms with us, and then they will go to the local bar to discuss their experience. If we know people want to go to the bar in addition to playing a game with us, we highly encourage them to go to the bar afterwards rather than before. However, sometimes they go to the bar in advance of checking in with us. The following are stories of some of the groups that stood out coming to Great Escape intoxicated.

Stumbling through the front door of our business, a group of couples enter. They just came from King's Table and were noticeably drunk. We do reserve the right to not play a group if any of its participants are a danger to our staff members or to the group itself. However, they were playing the Bank Vault, which is our most secure room and has the least amount of stuff that could break, or so I thought. Reading rules to a group of drunken adults is like having a conversation with my two-year-old nephew. My nephew might make eye contact with me and even occasionally smile to show that he understands me, but he has no clue what I'm saying to him. Drunken people aren't too different. They will nod their heads, smile, crack a joke or two, and even try to convince me that they are paying attention. However, they usually don't listen to a word I have said, and that was no different with this group.

From the first five minutes of the game this group was being destructive. One girl in the group took out all of the drawers to the desk and filing cabinet in the room and placed the drawers in the opposite corners. Another girl was trying to take a selfie in the room with her boyfriend. We don't mind the selfies, just not in the room! This is top-secret stuff after all. About halfway through the game I had taken my attention away from the monitor for about two seconds. When I looked back, there was a guy dangling from the rope that is hanging from the ceiling in the room. This rope is eight feet in the air. How the heck did this drunken guy get up there? Anyway, he let go of the rope before I got a chance to come over the microphone to tell him to please place both feet on the ground.

Toward the end of the game, one of the couples started arguing. The woman was giving the guy a hard time for not listening to her, or maybe it was for something else he did. I'm not really sure because I wasn't listening to her. Just kidding of course! They continued arguing, and then the guy walked over to a somewhat large cabinet on the wall, lifted the cabinet, and proceeded to walk around the room with it. In horror, I watched as a $400 cabinet was being hauled around the room by some random guy that had one-too-many shots of Johnnie Walker Black (accept no substitutes). Luckily, I was able to calm him down, and I convinced him to put the cabinet back on the wall. The fun didn't stop there though.

Throughout the Bank Vault experience, players find money and valuables. Near the end of the game, two of the guys took the money that they had collected so far, opened the door to the Bank Vault, and started roaming the hallways of my establishment, yelling as if they had just won the lottery. I ran out of the game master room to track these two individuals down before they randomly opened the doors to another one of our escape rooms that was in progress. I got to them in time and shuffled them back into their room. When it was all said and done, the group did terribly and barely made it halfway through the puzzles and clues. At least all the group members had a good time though—that is, until their hangovers kicked in the next day.

Having people come in to play a game after having a drink or two from King's Table is quite common. Most of the time, the individuals who come from there or come tipsy from another bar don't cause too much trouble. If anything, the tipsier a person is, the funnier he or she can be in the room.

The most outrageous group to ever come through the Great Escape Game drunk was a group of couples consisting of people around 30 years old. They played the Egyptian Tomb on the latest time slot. This was during our first year in business, when the latest game was at 10:30 p.m. When they entered the lobby, they told me right off the bat that they were going to be a fun group, and they didn't disappoint.

At Great Escape we always go over the rules with players before putting them into the room. This normally takes about two-to-three minutes. However, it took about 10 minutes to get through the rules with this rambunctious crowd. After going over the rules, I guided the players into the room and started their experience. I wasn't prepared for the next 60 minutes, but I'm not sure they were either. Inside the Egyptian Tomb there is an eight-foot-tall statue of the Egyptian God Anubis. Before bringing groups into the room we tell the players that the statue is not a part of the game and that they don't need to touch it. To reinforce this rule, we wrote do not touch on the statue itself (in gold paint of course). Within the first five minutes of the game I had to ask the group to not touch Anubis, as they were climbing on the statue. I told them to please not touch the Egyptian figure, but one of the girls insisted that she wanted to dance with the mythical strong man and begin doing so. Luckily, she stopped and got down before any damage was done to her or my statue.

Later in the game, they found a skull that is in one of the boxes. For the next couple of minutes, I watched in amusement as everyone took turns performing his or her best Hamlet impression. Imagine karaoke plus acting, but in an escape room and with no music, and that was what I was treated to. After the Shakespeare act, the players found a leather belt with some letters on it that are used in combination with another object to solve a riddle. Upon finding this belt, a guy in the group took the long piece of leather and started whipping his girlfriend with it. One would think this fun playful banter would end after a whip or two, but one would be wrong. Next thing you know, all the girls were lining up and putting their legs up on a pedestal in the room to get whipped. It was like a firing squad in there. The guys were all passing the leather belt around to each other and were taking turns whipping the girls in the room. I'm not sure if I was watching an escape room or the next edition of college Girls Gone Wild. The lashings finally subsided, and the room returned to normal but only for a short while.

Next thing I know, two guys in the room have their girlfriends on their shoulders, and each of these girls is trying to knock the other off her boyfriend's shoulders. One girl, while propped up in the air, discovered the microphone in the ceiling that allows us to hear the players in the room and proceeded to repeatedly tap on it, at which point I made the mistake of asking her to stop tapping on the ceiling microphone. My request for the reduction of noise made the girl tap harder on the microphone and even start yelling in it. I was near the point of threatening to end the group's game, before the girl finally got down from her boyfriend's shoulders. The next 15 minutes or so went by in a relatively normal manner, with only an occasional drunken outburst from a group member or two.

The group was down to the last 10 minutes of the game, when the unthinkable happened. One of the girls in the room took off her shirt. I wish that the story would just end there, but it didn't. Next thing I know the shirtless woman started calling my name, saying she wanted me to come into the Tomb to give her a kiss. For the next five minutes, she insisted that I come into the room, and then her bra came off! It was kind of crazy, especially because there were five other people in the room with her, none of which said a word about her actions or seemed to think that it was out of the ordinary. What's more out of place is one of the guys in the room was her boyfriend! With three minutes on the clock the girl decided it was best that she get it together and put her shirt back on. The group failed miserably, of course, and opted out of the end-of-game picture. They all left happy, and I was left wondering what the heck I just saw. Friendly reminder to all of you lovebirds out there that our rooms are recorded both visually and audibly! For that woman's privacy and that of the group I deleted the corresponding video immediately after the game.

Although it is common to have people come from the bar next door before playing an escape room, seeing a group whose members are drunk or very tipsy isn't a common occurrence. Outside of individuals being tipsy are the groups of people that come high on marijuana. I'm not condoning or recommending what people should do or not do in their private lives; however, I must point out that these individuals that come in high are almost always late to their games, and when they arrive you know they are high immediately. I'm not here to debate the effects of getting high or whether anyone should or shouldn't do it. For me, what people want to do in their time is their business. If you want to beat an escape room, however, you are better off not coming in with the munchies. In virtually every game I've watched in which the individuals are high, they lose. Not only do they fail, but also, they are so bad that they usually don't get close to finishing. This isn't because they get dumber or any nonsense like that. What sticks out to me the most is the speed at which they play the game. There is never any sense of urgency in their actions when they are in a room. I can come over the microphone, tell them what they need to do, make it apparent that they need to do it quickly, and that won't change the speed at which they attempt to accomplish the goal. There is one speed when someone is high from weed, and that speed is called chill. Again, this isn't me judging or even caring if someone gets high before playing an escape room, it's just my observation after watching dozens of escape rooms in which the players come in high.

On occasion, I will observe an individual in a room that, even without the backing of alcohol or another substance that gets them high, is still absolutely hopeless. This person might seem to be taking on a passive role in the experience, but some of the time I believe he or she simply does not know what's going on. These players kind of drag themselves into the room and, once inside, find a corner or wall to hole up. Sometimes they are under the weather or have just started arguing with their significant other. Other times the players might have had a long week or been busy at work prior to coming out. Having a passive or hopeless individual happens every couple of weeks or so and isn't that common of an occurrence. However, every full moon the passive players multiply and come into the Great Escape Game as one unit: a room packed full of people that seem like they just came from a casting of a popular zombie television show. These players really don't stand a chance when they walk into our rooms and, from what I can tell, don't seem to care anyway.

This group of hopeless individuals can be spotted before it is put into the room, as the individuals are usually painful to interact with. It's hard to pinpoint exactly why some groups do so terribly, but they seem to feed on each other's hopelessness. If one person in the room gives off the hopelessness vibe, or mutters some words of bleakness, I notice that negative energy can transfer to the others in the group. Just like the story of the bad apple.

A hopeless individual, or bad apple, left to him or herself will rot, and that will be that. However, place that hopeless person in a room, or bag if you'd like, and the decay spreads throughout, restraining all forms of confidence and optimism.

OBSERVATION 12

Be ready and focused for what life throws your way.

CHAPTER THIRTEEN

Liar, Liar, Pants on Fire

"If you tell the truth,
you don't have to remember anything."
−MARK TWAIN−

A notification on my phone went off; it was a negative Facebook review. The individual had given us a rating of three stars out of five. If it isn't five stars I leap into action like a superhero when crime strikes. In the review the individual complained that this was her least favorite escape room. She went on to say that she was paired with teenagers and that her game master was unhelpful and rude. Hold the phone. Did she call one of my employees rude? If someone didn't have a good experience in our escape room, that's ok. We strive to help everyone escape reality and do our best to make the experience enjoyable for everyone. Eventually there will be people that don't like escape rooms, and that's ok. However, what I don't have are rude or unprofessional employees. Keep in my mind that we have visual and audio recording of all our rooms and our lobby. This means that I can monitor a customer's journey with us from the moment he or she walks into the door until the moment he or she walks out. The Great Escape Game was rather busy the day I received the negative review; so, I didn't get a chance to review the tape until the next morning, but I did respond right away and apologize to her for not having a good time. I also mentioned that we pride ourselves on customer service and that I was surprised to hear that one of our game masters acted in a manner that was unprofessional.

When I reviewed the recordings of her game, my main concern was to see if my employees acted in a manner that they shouldn't have. This lady and her husband were paired up with a couple of teenagers and making sure the younglings weren't misbehaving was also a concern. I watched the entire hour of her game, which included going over the rules, the game itself, and the interaction between the players and the game master. Toward the end of the game the lady who had written the review did start to appear to be getting agitated on the video but seemed to be having fun throughout the experience. I didn't witness or hear anything from the teenagers that would be considered annoying. The game ended, and our manager walked into the room to tell them that they were all busted because time had run out. Upon entering, the game master was smiling and cheerful. The game master also encouraged all of the players by telling them they did a great job and then asked if everyone had fun, to which the entire group, including the lady who wrote the bad review, said yes. The game master brought the group to the lobby, took their picture, and thanked them for coming out. To quote my game master: "Thank you all for coming out. It was my pleasure to be your game master."

My employee was amazing (I never had any doubt that she would be). At this point, Ms. Liar, Liar, Pants on Fire had responded to my original response and written that my only competitor in Dayton would inform them if the group with which it was being paired consisted of any players whom were kids. This is a flat out lie. I responded that I had played all of my competitor's rooms and had been paired with strangers on all occasions, half of which were with teenagers. Not once was I informed at my local competitor's business, or at any of the 30 different rooms I've played across North America, of my group being paired with teenagers in the room or of any other demographics of the other players for that matter. I also said I reviewed the tape and that it appeared that we acted in a manner of friendliness, honesty, and professionalism.

Ms. Liar, Liar, Pants on Fire responded by saying she had played eight other rooms, that the staff at that business had let her know every time if there were going to be children in the room, and that this wasn't as enjoyable as the other three rooms she's done. What a minute I thought she's done eight rooms? Now I was starting to get confused. (Anyone reading this book that has done an escape room knows that escape room businesses don't let you know the age of the other participants in the room). This is where I should have just let it go and moved on. However, I don't like being lied to, especially about my employees; so, I called my competitor to whom this lady was referring and asked the staff person answering the phone if her employer allows the staff to tell customers the ages of the individuals in the group that will be paired with the customer's group. She stated that she doesn't have a way of knowing the personal information of the players in the room and that her employer does not allow staff to give any details about a group or its individuals to a paired group except the number of players in that paired group.

I responded back to Ms. Liar, Liar, Pants on Fire's review and let her know that I had called the other escape room and was informed that they don't tell customers the ages of the other players. She responded that she has been told twice that there would be kids joining her group in the room and that the other escape rooms were a lot more professional. First, it was eight games that told her kids would be in the room, then it was three games, and now it's two. I responded that I wished we could resolve the miscommunication and that we hoped that we would see her again. She responded that it was not likely and that she should have given us a lower review than what she did. I finally left it alone, something I should have done several responses earlier.

Months later, I was at the Great Escape Game working on a couple of different projects. One of my tasks for that evening was to go through all of the reviews we had to make sure there wasn't something on there that wasn't addressed. I stumbled on the review from Ms. Liar, Liar, Pants on Fire, reviewed it, and moved on. What happened next is almost unbelievable. About an hour after going through all the reviews guess who strolls through the door? It was Ms. Liar, Liar, Pants on Fire and her husband! I couldn't believe it. It was six months past the time she said she wasn't going to come back into my business, and I had just reread her review before she walked in.

I gave them my normal welcome speech and then asked them if they have ever done an escape room before. Without missing a beat, Ms. Liar, Liar, Pants on Fire said no! I was laughing inside. What were the odds of me looking at her review right before she came in? They ended up playing the Outbreak room with strangers, and I had someone else be their game master. The group escaped with under a minute to go. The players rushed out of the room and were high fiving each other. Smiles were on everyone's faces. They had beaten the second hardest room the Great Escape has to offer; so, why not celebrate? I took the group's picture and, since they beat the game, asked them if they wanted to buy our exclusive "I Escaped" t-shirt, which can only be bought if players beat their scenario. Most of the group didn't want to buy one, but guess who did purchase one? That's right, Ms. Liar, Liar, Pants on Fire bought a t-shirt. How funny is that? While she was in the game, I went back to confirm that was in fact the lady who wrote the terrible review, and it was. At that point, I knew her name, and when the credit card was processing for her t-shirt purchase, I asked her by name if her experience with the Outbreak was better than last time in the Bank Vault. She and her husband just looked down at the desk and didn't answer me. They finalized the transaction and left as happy customers that night. I still wonder to this day if her pants are still burning.

About two months after Ms. Liar, Liar, Pants on Fire came in to play her first game, I had a family of four play the Tomb. The family consisted of a mom, dad, son, and daughter. The children were around the ages of nine and 10. This was the first time any of the family members had played an escape game, and the kids were very excited to play. I gave them some bonus hints prior to entering the Tomb and then put them in the room. I don't remember much of their experience, but I do remember that they had failed.

Three months later, I received a notification of a customer review that was one star out of five. The mother in the family I mentioned above had written the review and stated that she had a terrible experience, it wasn't worth the money, and that she wouldn't recommend it to anyone. Concerned, I looked her up in our customer database to find the game and watch video of it. I found the individual quickly in our system, got the date and time that she played the room, and went back to the game master room to watch the film. While reviewing her video, I noticed that I was the game master for her and her family. The individuals playing the game didn't do well in the room. I ended up giving the group five hints instead of the traditional three, but it couldn't save them from the curse of the Pharaoh. After their time had expired, I walked into the room and told them that they were all cursed. Everyone in the room laughed. I asked what they thought about the Egyptian Tomb. The kids both screamed that they wanted to play another game, the mother said she had a lot of fun, and the dad told me that it was hard but seemed happy about his experience. I covered the things that they did right and showed them what they had to do to finish the game. After I finished my end-of-game speech, the dad said, "This was awesome."

After reviewing the tape, I was perplexed as to why we received a one-star rating. I looked up the contact information of the individual who wrote the bad review and gave her a call. I told her I was the owner of the Great Escape

Game and that I had received her review and watched her game again. I asked her to tell me about her experience. She informed that she thought the experience was overpriced and that she didn't have a good time. I followed up with a couple of open-ended questions to get her talking about the reason she had a bad time aside from the price. Finally, the truth came out. Apparently one of the kids started throwing a fit after they left and was upset that they hadn't passed the room. I was sympathetic with her, and I apologized that she didn't have the experience she wanted. I stressed the importance of our reviews and mentioned that it appeared as though everyone had a great time in the room, to which she replied, "You deal with upset kids, and then we'll talk," and then hung up on me. The weird thing about this story is that her review came more than three months past the date when she and her family came into our business.

Throughout the video of her game, everyone was happy and excited. Even in the after-game picture everyone is smiling ear to ear. Why go out of your way to write a bad review because your kids were upset after the fact? I never did figure out why this individual decided to write a bad review months after what appeared to be a good experience with us. The most confusing part was the fact this individual lied about having a good time and refused to acknowledge anything good from the experience solely because her children go upset. From that moment on, I tried my hardest to make sure that every group with kids would pass our escape rooms.

OBSERVATION 13

Ask yourself this question before doing anything:
Will my actions or words be a positive force in the universe?

CHAPTER FOURTEEN

Getting Involved in the Game

*"Focus on the journey,
not the destination. Joy is found
not in finishing an activity
but in doing it."*
—GREG ANDERSON—

In my opinion, the best way to get the most out of playing an escape game is to immerse yourself as much as possible into the experience. We try to make that easy at the Great Escape Game, by creating and purchasing props and puzzles that are related to the overarching theme of the room. Our goal is that when customers step inside our rooms, they feel like they are a part of that scenario. When the players get involved, it makes it more fun for them as well as the game masters watching the rooms.

I remember watching one group of teenage girls play our Area D room. Throughout the experience the girls were playing the roles of military members. There are several games in Area D that offer realistic military gadgets and props that help enable this environment of fun. The girls would put on the Air Force jackets found in the room and salute each other during the game. Instead of walking around the room, they would march in a line singing a recent pop song in unison (don't ask me what song it was). I would try to keep them on track and gave them small clues throughout the game. They played the game decently, but, in the end, they got themselves blown up. While the final seconds ticked on the three televisions in the room, the girls huddled together ready to embrace their fate. With fake tears in their eyes they said their last goodbyes and passed away in each other's arms. I came into the room with a smile on my face. They had failed Area D, but if you saw their expressions and felt their energy, you would have thought they set the record in the room. They didn't care whether they'd won or not; they just wanted to have fun, and that's exactly what they did.

A similar story occurred in the Bank Vault that same month. A group of friends came in to play a room. The friends had never played an escape room before but were excited to give it a go. This was a fun group, and everyone was talking about what he or she was going to do when he or she found the loot from the bank. One individual was going to buy a fancy sports car. Another person was going to disappear and head to Mexico with his newly acquired fortune. The players were ready to begin; so, I brought them to the room and started going over the rules with them. The last thing I go over with groups is how to win the game, and I mentioned that if they don't get the loot and escape the room within an hour, they would all be arrested. One of the players turned to his friend and said, "He might like that too much." Everyone began laughing, while I just shook my head and started their experience.

Throughout the hour a voice meant to sound like a police scanner comes over the sound system to make the game more realistic. The first voice over the loudspeaker alerts officers to the bank alarm being tripped and shut off and requests a police drive by. With 10 minutes left in the game a panicked voice comes over the sound system that states, "All available officers to H&K Banking for a code three. Robbery is in progress. I repeat, all available officers to H&K Banking for a code three." At this point all of the players, nearly in unison, raised their hands in the air in the "Don't shoot" position and kept them there until finally I came over the microphone to tell them they could put their hands down. I was cracking up watching them play. After this message stating that a robbery is in progress, the music plays in the background a little more intensely, which is designed to get players' hearts racing. When the timer has only two minutes left, the screen starts flashing, and police sirens begin playing in the background. With 30 seconds left in the game, and with the sirens getting louder, all six players in the room lined up and put their hands on one of the walls. I couldn't stop laughing and figured by the time I walked over to the room to let them know they failed they would be in a normal stance. This was not the case. As I walked in the room the players were still on the wall, and not one of them turned to look up at me. I stood there in the room, and they all had their heads looking down, feet spread. I wasn't sure if they were involved in theatre or had real world experience in this situation, but the result was still the same. I was smiling ear to ear. Finally, one of the guys broke stance and walked up to me with his hands together like he was expecting to get cuffed. I couldn't stop laughing. Even after the group left, I was smiling. The players didn't come into the Great Escape Game wanting to fail; however, even though they didn't pass, they made the best of it and, in turn, had an awesome time. The best part is they made my entire day better.

OBSERVATION 14

Sometimes you just gotta have some fun.

WILL THEY ESCAPE?

CHAPTER FIFTEEN

Oh, No He Didn't

"Love is a lot like a backache. It doesn't show up
on x-rays, but you know it's there."
—GEORGE BURNS—

I was at work one Wednesday afternoon waiting for the 4:30 p.m. Egyptian room time slot to start. The time was now 4:30 p.m., and the group had not arrived yet. I pulled up the customer information and gave them a call. A gentleman picked up the phone, and I introduced myself and told him I had him down for a 4:30 p.m. game at our establishment. He apologized and informed me that he and his fiancé got into a fight. Apparently, the fight resulted in her getting out of the vehicle, and she was now roaming around the streets of Beavercreek, Ohio, where my business is located. I felt bad for the guy and offered to reschedule his experience at no extra charge. The gentleman thanked me for the offer but said that the other half of his group would be coming in to play the game in the next five minutes and would still play. I got off the phone with him and waited for the two individuals to arrive. A few minutes later, three of the original four arrived at the Great Escape Game ready to play the Tomb. I asked about the fourth individual to determine if she would eventually be joining the three players. Apparently, the girl who had gotten out of the truck and her fiancé live more than a two hours' drive away, and she was still wandering around the streets. The guy with the missing fiancé suggested that the other couple start the game while he attempted to find her. The couple agreed, and I took them back to the room.

Our games are extremely difficult when there are only two people in the room; so, I told them I would give them some extra hints to help them out. I put the couple into the Egyptian Tomb and started their game. I wasn't expecting to see the guy with the missing fiancé again. Thirty minutes into the game, guess who strolls through the front door and into the lobby? The guy and his fiancé! I took them to the room, went over the rules of the game quickly, and then opened the door to the Tomb. Imagine giving rules to two individuals that just got into an argument big enough to convince one of them to get out of a vehicle—all while being two hours from home to which you can't easily get an Uber. Long story short, they didn't hear a word I said. Without any more delay, I put them in the room. I was dreading watching the rest of the game. The tension between the fighting couple was so obvious you could feel it. Why they thought it was a good idea to go into an escape room together after all that was beyond me, but they did.

When I made it back to the game master room I was glued to that monitor, watching the fighting couple's every move. Without much time having passed, the couple began fighting again. It got so bad that it seemed like I was watching a bad reality TV show. I hate to admit that I started to enjoy the show, but I did. I was desperately looking for some popcorn to eat so that I could lean back and appreciate watching the game like I would a movie (think Michael Jackson in the music video Thriller). The fighting couple didn't even play the game. The woman in the room had her arms crossed the entire time, and the guy was getting so upset that I could his face turning red. Keep in mind that the lighting in the Tomb is not normal, and the illumination in the room produces an orange-reddish glow to make the experience more realistic. The fighting couple held it together for the next 20 minutes, and then it happened. "You're such a b***h." I perked up in my chair like I just got pinched. I'm 90 percent certain my mouth was wide open as I just stared at the monitor expecting World War III to begin in front of my very own eyes. Surprisingly, the woman just shook her head and moved to a different part of the room. I have to give her mad props because if I were she, I would have jumped on him like a spider monkey and reigned terror upon him.

Luckily the game was almost over, and after two more minutes the game was finished. With hesitation, and ready to defend myself against any random acts of aggression, I walked into the room. I tried as hard as I could to defuse the situation by talking about all the great things the group had accomplished and figured out on its own. I made eye contact with everyone, told the players they did awesome, and congratulated them on almost finishing. They were nowhere near completing the room, but I didn't have the heart to tell them that. I wanted there to be some positive vibes from my business. I walked them out to the lobby and told them to get underneath the key to get their picture taken on our photo wall. Yeah, that didn't happen. Everyone ran out of the Great Escape Game faster than a mouse when it sees a cat. I can only imagine how awkward that drive home had to have been.

OBSERVATION 15

Never go to bed or enter an escape room angry.

WILL THEY ESCAPE?

CHAPTER SIXTEEN

High-Schoolers: You Never Know What You're Going to Get

"Please, God, please, don't let me be normal!"
−SIGOURNEY WEAVER−

It is important that the game masters know exactly where the players are timewise in a room. A delay on our end regarding giving a hint to the players could mean the difference between whether or not a group passes or fails. There are microphones in every room, and our game masters have on headsets to ensure that we can always hear our groups. We have cameras located in every single hallway, escape room, and game master room, as well as two in the main lobby. We can see and hear everything that goes on within our walls. We've seen and heard some interesting things at the Great Escape Game. However, some of the most interesting groups to watch are high schoolers. You never know what you are going to get with them.

While most high schoolers are fun and enjoyable to watch, there was one group I can recall that was the opposite of fun. This group had been spawned in the underworld itself, and from the moment the players entered the lobby they were being rude and obnoxious. This group was playing the Outbreak and refused to listen to anything I said while I was going over the rules. Regardless, I finished with the instructions, brought all of the players into the room, started the video, and wished them good luck.

The group was struggling for the first 10 minutes; so, I came over the microphone and gave them a small hint to push them in the right direction.

While I was giving the hint, one of the girls in the room (we'll call her Ms. Too Cool for School) looked at the camera and gave me the bird. It was the first and only time a player had done that. I came over the microphone and told that young girl to please not do that again. Have you ever told a high schooler to not do something? How did that go for you? The girl responded to my request by leaning back and using both hands to make a chopping motion to her crotch. I was speechless at that point. Play continued, and I hoped that the players would focus on trying to solve the puzzles again. About 20 minutes later the players got into the second room of the Outbreak game.

Inside the second room there is a dry-erase board for players to write on. Upon entering the room Ms. Too Cool for School decided to write "Our game master is a peice of s**t" on the dry-erase board. The minions in the room all laughed and danced around like they won the Super Bowl. While I did find it amusing that she spelled the word piece wrong, I didn't find her writing that on the board to be appropriate. I came over the microphone and told her to erase it. Everyone in the room, except one, started hooting and hollering. Ms. Too Cool for School responded by walking up to the camera and giving me the bird again.

For the entire game Ms. Too Cool for School, and most of the group, were being destructive and rude. However, there was one girl in the group that was very nice and was really into the game. If the enjoyable adolescent hadn't been in the room, I would have ended the group's game early and told the players to leave my establishment. However, it wasn't fair to the one pleasant youngster in the room to terminate the game. Ms. Too Cool for School was constantly complaining throughout the experience, and near the end of the game, with eyes and body directed at the camera she jerked her chest out and her arms back in a single lunging motion as one would in a "Come at me, bro" manner. The game finally ended. The group had failed. I went into the room, encouraged them with a "Job well done," and brought them to the lobby. Ms. Too Cool for School didn't make eye contact with me once.

At the end of the escape game, players hold up two signs. The first sign shows what room they played, and the second sign shows their escape time or displays that they "almost escaped." I usually hand them the room sign first and make sure everyone is in position before I hand them the second sign. I do this because I feel it's a little more dramatic. My approach with this group was no different. I handed them the game room sign, and when everyone was ready, I handed them the sign that says, "Almost escaped." The lone agreeable Miss in the group smiled, and everyone else groaned in disapproval. Ms. Too Cool for School didn't find it amusing, rolled her eyes, and whispered something under her breath. After the picture, I asked everyone if he or she had fun. I got several different negative responses ranging from no to "It was boring." Of course, Ms. Too Cool for School couldn't leave that question alone and responded with "No, this place sucks." They all left, and I just stood there wondering what the heck just went down. While this group was terrible, it's important to note that not all high schoolers are rude like this. Some groups of high schoolers can be a lot of fun. The next story is a prime example of the creativity of young adults.

The energy of high-schoolers seems to be unlimited, as all of you parents out there with high-schoolers can attest to, and their creativity can go unmatched. I remember putting in a group of high schoolers into the Outbreak room one weekend, and these teens couldn't focus to save their lives. Eventually I made it through the rules, and they started the game.

Within five minutes one of the kids had drawn something inappropriate on the dry-erase board on the wall. Everyone in the room laughed, while I sat in the game master room shaking my head. Shortly after, the funniest sequence of events that has ever happened to me at Great Escape occurred. I got dabbed on by one of the high school kids. A dab is where you drop your head into your bent arm while raising the opposite arm out straight, parallel with the ground. Although he didn't start it, the dab became famous when football player Cam Newton started doing it after first downs and touchdowns back in October of 2015. This wasn't just a dab to anyone though; it was geared toward me only. Before the first dab took place, the individual yelled at me to take notice of him. He wanted me to see it. Staring at the camera for a couple of seconds while time seemed to stand still, he dabbed on me. I wasn't sure if he was being silly or challenging my superiority; so, I let the dabbing go on. Each time the team solved a puzzle or clue the individual would come to the same camera, stare at it for a couple seconds, and then would dab on me. This continued throughout the entire game.

At the end of the experience the players found the item that would allow them to escape the laboratory. While six high schoolers ran from one room to the next to escape, one was left behind. It was he. Staring into the camera. Staring into my soul. Everyone else had already left the room and was celebrating in the hallway, but not this kid. He sat there and watched, and gaped, and gawked, and finally in a moment of triumph, he dabbed one last time. I smile to this day when I think of how funny that kid was.

OBSERVATION 16

Embrace the fun and creativity of teenagers.

CHAPTER SEVENTEEN

We've Been Robbed

"Lying and stealing are next-door neighbors."
-PROVERBS-

I had a group of my friends book the Bank Vault one Friday evening, and I decided to come into the Great Escape Game to say hello and make sure everything was perfect for their game. When I got to work, I noticed that the front desk was a little messy. I started to organize the desk and moved things around to where they should be. I came across something on the desk that needed to go into the filing cabinet under the desk. Upon opening the bottom drawer of the filing cabinet, I noticed something strange. Inside this drawer we keep a small locked safe that contains several $5 bills. We use the safe as a backup if we run out of money in our cash box. On top of the desk we have an open cash box that has around $25 worth of fives in it. In order to book an escape room with us you must use a credit card. You can't book a game with cash, but you can use it to buy a t-shirt. It costs $15 to buy one of our "I Escaped" t-shirts, and people often pay with $20. We use these fives for change when someone purchases a t-shirt. If, for someone reason, we run out of $5 bills in the open cash box on the desk, the manager on duty can open the small safe in the filing cabinet to get more fives.

When I opened the bottom drawer of the filing cabinet the small safe was open. I tried to lock it, and to my confusion it wouldn't lock. I discovered that the safe wouldn't latch because it had a huge dent in it. I was trying to figure out how the safe could have been busted open like that. I sent a picture of it to my business partner Mike, and within 30 minutes he came up to the Great Escape Game. While I was clueless as to how the safe could have gotten this huge depression in it, Mike knew exactly what had happened and informed me that someone forced his or her way into the safe. To prove it, he put the safe on the ground and stood on top of the safe with all his weight. Nothing happened to the safe from him standing on it. At that moment, I realized that he was right. This was no accident; someone must have forced his or her way into the moneybox.

I knew the break-in had to have occurred in the past five days because on Monday of the same week, my business partner had gone to the bank and withdrawn 150 dollars' worth in five-dollar bills, and at 4:00 p.m. that day I had opened the small safe and placed this 150 dollars' worth of five-dollar bills inside. After placing the money in the safe, I locked it, put it back into the bottom drawer, and went about my day. Mike and I went back to one of the game master rooms and started watching the video recordings of the lobby, starting with the recordings from Monday at 4:00 p.m. We were watching the tape for about an hour when our manager walked into the game master room to see what we were doing. We showed her the damaged safe, and she mentioned that last night she was in the area and stopped by the Great Escape Game around 8:30 p.m. She said that when she walked into the lobby, she saw the employee on shift (we'll call him Mr. Lapse of Judgment) messing around with something on the bottom drawer of the black filing cabinet. This was bizarre to her because she knew that nothing was down there except for the safe. Mr. Lapse of Judgment stated that he was simply organizing the drawers, and the manager reminded him to not play around at work because Mike and I watch everything that goes on. She then left the building.

This bit of information was helpful to us because watching five days of footage would have taken a long time. We started a new video recording search for that Thursday starting at 8:00 p.m. It didn't take long before we saw what we didn't want to. Mr. Lapse of Judgment was sitting at the desk, and then all the sudden he grabbed a screwdriver that he brought from the back room and started working on prying open the safe. He was working on opening the safe for about five minutes before our manager arrived. The crazy part of it is that when watching our manager's interaction with Mr. Lapse of Judgment, we saw her point to the camera and then she said, "Don't dick around. Mike and Danny can see you." At this stage in the process you would think that after your boss comes in and almost busts you breaking into the safe, all while pointing at the camera that is less than 10 feet away, you would shape up and stop the attempted robbery. This was not the case.

Ten minutes after the manager left the Great Escape Game Mr. Lapse of Judgment was back at it. For the next 15 minutes he pried and pried, trying as hard as he could to open the safe. Finally, he placed the safe on the ground and stomped on it. The safe was now open. He picked up the now open box and put it on the desk. There was $150 in the safe. Initially, Mr. Lapse of Judgment put the entire stack of cash in his pocket. After a minute, he decided it would be better to leave behind $35 of the $150 and put the broken safe back in the drawer. Mr. Lapse of Judgment then left for the night.

The craziest part of this whole ordeal is that there are two cameras in the lobby. We can see every angle in the business. Mr. Lapse of Judgment knew that we watch the tapes frequently, and he and I have reviewed video footage together in the past. On top of that, our manager told him in the middle of his heist that we are watching and pointed to the camera that was facing him. It wasn't easy to watch Mr. Lapse of Judgment steal from the business. I consider all of my employees a part of my extended family; so, when Mr. Lapse of Judgment stole from me, it was like a member of my own blood stealing from me. To make things worse, Mr. Lapse of Judgment came to work the very next day like nothing had happened. After reviewing the tape, I asked Mr. Lapse of Judgment to follow me to one of the game masters rooms because I had to talk to him. I brought him into the game master room and hit play on the tape. We started watching the video, and then I asked him what he was doing in the tape. We both stood there in silence for what seemed like forever. At that point, he wasn't saying anything; so, I told him if he tells me what he is doing, then I will be nice to him. Finally, he summoned the strength to speak and said, "I'm stealing from you." I then asked him to give me his work key and told him he is no longer an employee at the Great Escape Game. Since he was honest with me, I promised not to call the cops on him. He gave me his key and left the building.

I was devastated. Not only because he had stolen from me but also because he was going through a rough spot in his life. He had just gotten out of jail about two months ago for something minor and hadn't been able to get back on his feet since getting out. The weekend prior to the theft his girlfriend had kicked him out, and he had had no place to live. He had been written up twice in the past two weeks for non-theft-related incidents, but I kept giving him chances because he was related to a good friend of mine. At this point in my life I had started five businesses and I have had to let go several people in the past seven years of entrepreneurship. Letting Mr. Lapse of Judgment go was one of the hardest to do. I knew by watching the video that his actions were a result of sheer desperation, and I sympathized with that. When he walked out that door he would have nowhere to go, no job, and his previous criminal record. In the end, the result would have always been the same; however, I'll always wonder what I could have done differently to prevent his actions on that fateful Thursday night. He knew we were watching, and that didn't stop him. Although we were watching him on the tape, perhaps we should have been paying more attention to his life situation and behavior, then maybe we could have possibly made a difference.

OBSERVATION 17

Be fair, yet just.

CHAPTER EIGHTEEN

The Outbreak is Haunted

*"I don't believe in ghosts or paranormal activity, but one time
I think I saw—I might have seen—no, I think I did see a ghost."*

—JASON BLUM—

My business partner and I worked every single day in 2016, minus one week in March for vacation, before opening our escape room business and seven other random days of breaks. At the time prior to opening, we both worked other jobs and would go straight to the Great Escape Game and stay all night after we left our other employment. Our first mission was to get the lobby set up and then finish the Bank Vault. After both spaces were complete, we would work on completing the Outbreak room. After completing the Outbreak room we'd be ready to open our doors for business.

The construction of the lobby and the Bank Vault were accomplished quickly. After all, the Bank Vault is a very straight-forward room and didn't take much time for construction. The Outbreak room took a lot more time, as there were more detail and props in the room. One of the props in the Outbreak, which is one of my favorite props in any of our rooms, is a rotten corpse. This dead body was ordered from Dapper Cadaver, a Los Angeles-based company that specializes in professional-grade death, science, and Halloween props. The prop is called Rotten Ribs Alan, which features a dead body with exposed ribs, and depicts the state at which a body would be found after several weeks of decomposing. We were looking for a little wow factor when the players opened the body bag, and at a price of $900, Rotten Ribs Alan didn't disappoint. Rotten Ribs Alan, a body bag, and the table the body laid on were the first things we purchased for the Outbreak room. When the prop came in the mail, we carefully put it inside the body bag and placed both the bag and Rotten Ribs Alan on the examining table. At that point in the construction process, the only thing in the Outbreak room was a dead corpse and a lot of empty space.

The first couple of nights we left the body bag unzipped so that Rotten Ribs Alan could watch our progress in the room. One night, I had to go home from the Great Escape Game early, leaving my business partner Mike behind to work on the Outbreak. It was about 11:00 p.m. and Mike was working on installing a cabinet. The cabinet was on the opposite side of the room from Rotten Ribs Alan, and to work on the installation of the cabinet Mike had to have his back to the dead body. While installing the cabinet Mike said he heard the zipper move on the body bag. He quickly looked back and saw nothing out of the ordinary. The body bag is made from leather, and moments after hearing the zipper move, he heard the crease of the leather as if something had moved it. That was enough for Mike, as he bolted out of the room and called it quits for the evening. Perhaps it was late, and Mike was tired, which caused him to hear the things he did. Without a camera and microphone system setup yet, we were unable to go back to review the tape. There are probably several logical explanations of what happened in that room that night. However, what happened in the Outbreak 10 months after the body bag incident will spook me 'til the day I die.

The date was December 27, 2016. It was the end of the year and we had sold out every time slot in every room for the past and current week; we were booked solid for the next week as well. We didn't realize that at the end of the calendar year we would be so busy. We were short-staffed due to our unawareness of the potential to be sold out during this period, resulting in long hours for my business partner, my employees, and myself. Everyone was working overtime, and we were all exhausted. We only had four rooms at the time, and one game master room controlled all four experiences. Inside this game master space each room has its own monitor and station. The monitors are in the four corners of the game master room, which allows the game to be overseen by the game master with minimal distractions to the game masters of the other rooms. Inside the game master room were two employees, my business partner Mike, and me. I was watching a cursed group of tomb raiders in the Egyptian room, one employee was helping defuse a nuclear bomb in Area D, Mike was the getaway driver for the Bank Vault, and another employee was the chief medical scientist for the Outbreak.

We were all watching our respective games, when the employee watching the Outbreak, in a startled manner, said "What the heck?!" and leaped out of his chair, running into the hallway. He returned a couple of seconds later, and we asked him what was going on. The employee watching the Outbreak told us that he thought someone was drunk from the bar and was outside the Outbreak room messing with the door. However, when he had leapt out of his chair and ran into the hallway to tell that person to stop, there was no one there. We briefly looked at the hallway camera footage to see what was going on, but there was no one in the hallway. Everyone was too busy to continue looking at the footage, and we continued finishing the rest of the night's escape games. After the last game we decided to go back and review the hallway tape to see whom the troublemaker was in the hallway. Keep in mind, every single hallway and space at the Great Escape Game can be seen by a camera. There are no blind spots in our business. The hallway that is outside the Outbreak is more than 50 feet long, and there are no other doors or passageways. It is a straight shot from the game master room, past the Outbreak, and to the front door of the business.

The tape in the hallway revealed that the only individuals in the hallway were the players that were in the Outbreak room 50 minutes prior to the disturbance. We kept watching until the players finished the game and left the Outbreak. In the entire hour, not one person was in the hallway or even close to it. That was weird, but we didn't fully understand what had happened inside the room; so, we decided to review the tape of inside the Outbreak room. For the first 50 minutes of the replay of the game, nothing happened. Then, at 7:55 p.m. and 47 seconds, the unexplainable happened. The players were working on the last puzzle of the game, when, all the sudden, you could hear four knocks on the door: knock, knock, knock, knock. We didn't know what we were looking for at first, but after we heard the knocking, we rewound the tape and watched it again. One of the players was standing by the door facing the cabinet when all the sudden his head turns sharply toward the door. He appears to be staring at the door handle for almost three seconds and then says out loud to the group, "Hey hey," while continuing to stare at the door handle—and then it happens: knock, knock, knock, knock. Four knocks occur in succession on the door to the Outbreak room. The other players in the room look over at the door, and the kid next to the door says, "Someone is touching the door. Don't come in." The players shift their focus back on the puzzle they were trying to solve, and five minutes later they escape the Outbreak. We hit the rewind button and watched it again, this time focusing on the door and the kid. We couldn't see or hear anything at the door before the knocks, but the sharpness at which the kid turns his head is unmistakable. He heard something at that door, and it was loud enough to get him to turn his head and stare at the door for three seconds. Then came the knocking. The noise was loud and distinctive. Something outside of the Outbreak room was knocking on that door.

All our cameras in the building are linked to the exact same time. We pulled up the hallway camera and watched its footage of the same time frame that the knocking occurred on the door. There was no one there. A few moments later you see the employee that was watching the Outbreak on the hallway tape walk out to investigate the noise. I probably watched the video of the knocking a dozen times that night, and I couldn't wrap my head around it. I am not a superstitious person in the slightest and believe everything can be explained with reason and logic, but I couldn't figure this out. A strange knocking noise could be several different things, but it was more than that. That kid experienced something in addition to what we did, and I had to know what it was.

The next day, December 28, 2016, at noon, the same two employees from the night before and I decided to look up the contact information of the players in the room and gave them a call. When the individual picked up on the other end of the phone, we told him who we were and asked if he had played the Outbreak last night. He said he did play the Outbreak last night with some friends. At that point I asked him if anything out of the ordinary transpired while playing the game. He went on to tell me that during the game someone was scratching at the door to the room, and then someone knocked. The hairs stood up on the back of my neck. It was starting to add up. We had a ghost at the Great Escape Game. When the kid turned his head abruptly to look at the door, it was because he heard scratching on the door, and then he heard the knocking. I told him that we had reviewed the tapes several times, and there was no one in the hallway. He responded by telling us that paranormal activity was happening to the group all night after they had gotten home from Great Escape Game and that one of the group members got violently sick after the escape room.

The next week I probably watched the videos of the hallway and the Outbreak four dozen times. I tried my hardest to piece the puzzles together. Maybe it was just a random noise, but why did he look over at the door handle so convincingly? Why were there four knocks so loud and noticeable that every person in the room turned and looked at the door? Why did the group have paranormal activity happen to them all night after their experience? I couldn't explain what happened that night then, and I still can't to this day. What I do know is that I will remember that Tuesday and the ghost at the Great Escape Game for the rest of my life.

OBSERVATION 18

Some things are better left unexplained.

CHAPTER NINETEEN

Don't Actually Take the Treasure

"When there's a single thief, it's robbery.
When there are a thousand thieves, it's taxation."
−VANYA COHEN−

Sometimes it's just one or two actions that make a group a bad one. There were two couples playing the Tomb one night. They were on a double date and had done escape rooms before. Right off the bat, one of the guys was not listening and interrupted several times during the rules telling me how great he was at everything he did. This behavior continued from him throughout the rules and the entire game. The group did very well and beat the Egyptian Tomb with five minutes left. After the couples beat the room, they took their end-of-the-game picture and were on their way. I started to reset the room shortly after they left.

One of the first things I do when resetting the Tomb is put the Pharaoh's treasure back into the sarcophagus. I searched around the room without being able to locate that big shiny ruby that stays nestled in the Kings chamber. After a couple minutes, I decided to go back into the game master room to watch the tape and try to find the missing gem. Each game has its own recording box and camera system. This unit records all the audio and video of that game and stores it on a hard drive. It maintains this information for a several months and then it rewrites over itself with the new audio and video that is constantly being inputted as new games are played. I opened the recording system and played the video backward, starting from the end of the game. I found my missing ruby. The only problem was it was in the pocket of one of the guys in the group—the arrogant guy that was being a jerk had taken my ruby!

Watching the tape, this guy kind of smugly holds the ruby up to one of the cameras and then blatantly puts it in his pocket. I went to the front desk computer to get the information of the customer who had booked the room. I located the customer's number and called. A girl picked up the phone and I told her that it appeared that the guy with the backwards baseball cap (I can't make this stuff up) might have accidently placed the end-of-the-game ruby in his pocket. The girl placed me on hold and after a few moments came back and said that no one had anything in his or her pockets. I described the guy in the video again and explained to her that I watched it on the recording box. At that point she hung up on me. I called again to ask politely if the gentleman had found the game prop in his pocket. At that point one of the guys came on the phone and, rather aggressively, told me that I better stop calling. He then hung up the phone.

This ruby wasn't that big of an expense, but it was a matter of principle at that point. I called them again and left a voicemail stating that if I didn't get my game prop back by the end of the night, I would call the cops and press charges for theft. Thirty minutes later, guess who strolled through the door with my missing ruby? You guessed it! Mr. Jerk, himself. The crazy part is this guy started arguing with me about my behavior. He proceeded to tell me how much of a (insert bad word) I was and that he would never come to my establishment again. I was as calm as I could be during his tirade. Here's a guy that went out of his way to steal a game prop in my escape room, yells at me over the phone, hangs up on me, and then proceeds to blame me after he's been caught. It takes all kinds of people to make a world go 'round.

OBSERVATION 19

When you make a mistake in life, admit it,
apologize, and move forward in the right direction.

CHAPTER TWENTY

The Superstar in the Room is Right in Front of You, or Perhaps He or She is Behind You

"Hard work does not go unnoticed,
and someday the rewards will follow."
—ALLAN RUFUS—

A groups of individuals came into Great Escape Game as a team-building exercise for the company the group works for. The company's participants had already been divided into two teams before they arrived at Great Escape. The teams were doing an escape room as sort of a competition with each other. They had booked the Bank Vault, one of our easier rooms, and Area D, the hardest room available. Throughout conversation, the groups in the lobby discovered that Area D was much harder to beat than the Bank Vault. After a few more minutes of discussion, the players were ready to begin.

I brought my squad to the Area D rule poster. My team, now with the understanding that its room was the hardest of the six rooms we offered, was a little distraught and verbally expressed concern that not only would it not beat the other group, but it may not get out altogether. I reassured the group and was very careful to explain, in detail, all the tips and tricks they would need to know in order to pass the room. Out of all the things I stressed, communicating with the other members in the group was the most important, so significant that I made them all tell me they understood that communicating with everyone in the room was vital to their success. They nodded and confirmed that they got it and I walked them into the room.

The beginning of Area D is always interesting and, in many ways, a good indicator of how people will act throughout the game. The game begins with everyone handcuffed to the wall. They are not all in the same place in the nuclear hanger but rather scattered throughout the room at different locations. What this means is that all the potential bomb diffusers are within arm's reach of the key they need to get un-cuffed. The key could be located by a desk, a cabinet, piping, or the control panel that disarms the nuclear bomb, itself. When the game starts, there is sometimes one individual that is telling everyone in the room where the key must be, but often this person is wrong. This group had such a person in it. A gentleman that was right next to where the hidden key was located, shouted out commands, telling everyone where the key must be, all while not looking around his own vicinity. After minutes of struggling to find the key, I nudged the players in the right direction. They were free at last. Free from the handcuffs, that is. The threat of nuclear explosion was right around the corner if they didn't act fast.

The group started off quickly after getting out of the handcuffs, splitting up into two groups and doing a very good job searching through the room for their next clue. Maybe it was the knowledge that they were in the hardest room that put some speed behind them, or perhaps they knew they were already behind from being in the handcuffs so long. Either way they were finishing the first games with great speed. After completing the first couple of tasks, the team got stuck on a rather tricky game. The answer to this puzzle is right in front of them, but it can be difficult to decipher. A woman in the group (we'll call her Ms. Give Me a Chance), was working on a puzzle, when another individual in the group butted their way in and kind of kicked her aside. The group was struggling to finish this conundrum. At the same time, Ms. Give Me a Chance was pushed to the back of the crowd. I could hear her yell out how to solve the puzzle, but the individuals in front of her wouldn't listen to her. When they completed the puzzle, someone said, "That's what [Ms. Give Me a Chance] said to do." The look on her face was priceless.

The game moved forward until they got stuck on a series of clues that is easy once you know how to start it. Once again, Ms. Give Me a Chance was first to the scene, and once again Ms. Give Me a Chance got pushed off the game and was now in the back of the group. The players spent almost five minutes on this game. At least twice I could hear Ms. Give Me a Chance tell the members of her team how to start the puzzle. The group was forced to use a hint to figure out how to start the game. I would say Ms. Give Me a Chance's voice fell on deaf ears from the other members of the group, but once I told them how to do it, one of the individuals stated, "That's what [Ms. Give Me a Chance] was telling us to do." That was the second time in the game that someone in the group acknowledged that Ms. Give Me a Chance was right and knew what she was talking about. It's important to point out, at that stage of the game Ms. Give Me a Chance wasn't only right twice, but she was never wrong. If she didn't how to do something or how a game worked, she would say that she didn't know. Surely then, if in the last 11 minutes of the game Ms. Give Me a Chance said she knows how to do something, then the members of her group should listen to her. Right? Unfortunately, this was not the case.

With the last two pieces of the game in her hand Ms. Give Me a Chance knew she was onto something. She headed into the space where the final code was, and then the unthinkable happened. Someone grabbed the final pieces from her, strolled away from the spot they needed to be, and started walking around the room. The individual was thinking out loud, trying to figure out how these two components would help produce a code. With 2 minutes and 30 seconds left in the game Ms. Give Me a Chance told the individual that the two pieces probably go together, and they should go into the closet with it. Her words were ignored. Luckily for the group, it still had a hint left and used it just in the nick of time. They finished the room with 18 seconds left to spare.

I led the group to the lobby to get its end-of-the-game picture. I handed them the sign displaying to them that they played Area D and offered the poster that showed their cutting close time of 59:42. I attempted to hand this poster board to Ms. Give Me a Chance as I felt she earned the right to hold it, when someone else took it right out of my hand. The ending of this game made me feel bad for Ms. Give Me a Chance. I wasn't sure what was worse: the fact that the group had zero clue that she was the superstar in that room or watching her, while she was playing, become almost completely demotivated and uninspired by the fact that this group of her coworkers didn't listen to her. In this case, the superstar in the group was pushed aside and ignored. Without her, the group would have failed.

Ms. Give Me a Chance's situation can easily be blamed on men becoming a little forceful in certain situations, and in this case, there could be a small element of truth to that statement. However, I have seen the behavior of not listening to the person with all the answers multiple times, and a good number of them involve no male intervention. The next story occurred three weeks after Ms. Give Me a Chance's story and is a scenario in which there were only females in the room.

The teams were set and ready to take on the world upon entering. This wasn't a friendly competition between friends; it was war. The winners got bragging rights, and for this group of girls at that time, winning meant everything. The group consisted of members of a local high school girls' volleyball team, and they were there to win. The girls were playing without adults, and the coaches let us randomly assemble the players into four groups and decide which rooms the groups would play. We were prepared to begin the escape!

I was running the Area D room that day, and I led my group of volleyball players from the lobby towards the room to go over the rules with them. I explained the instructions and told them that they would be playing the hardest room we have. The girls were very attentive during the rules and were ready to play—and, most importantly, they were ready to win. I brought them into the escape room, handcuffed everyone to the wall, and played the video to start the game. The girls were funny to watch and were having a blast in the room. Progression in the room was at a normal rate, and they used their first hint when they realized they weren't getting anywhere.

Throughout the game I noticed something interesting. When the girls piled around something they were trying to figure out, they would always leave one girl behind them who couldn't see what was going on. We'll call her Ms. Superstar. The girls who could see the puzzles wouldn't tell Ms. Superstar in the back what they saw and didn't have much communication with her at all. This apparent lack of discussion with Ms. Superstar wasn't just in the beginning of the game; it continued throughout. Not too long after this, the girls were stuck on a puzzle. Ms. Superstar had a chance to see the puzzle before everyone else crowded around; so, she yelled from the back what to do, and it worked. Everyone was very excited and continued moving forward in the experience.

Minutes later, the girls got stuck on something in the room that has a secret lever. Seven girls huddled around this item, confused about what it did or how it opened. Again, from behind the pack of the competitive volleyball players, Ms. Superstar, seemingly left out of the group, shouted out what to do, and, again, it worked. Screams of joy and excitement filled the room again as high fives and hugs went around to everyone. Well almost everyone. Ms. Superstar produced all the answers and yet was left by herself without any high fives or hugs. This happened again for the third time with 15 minutes left in the game when the girls were confronted with a puzzle that is very hard to understand how to start. This time Ms. Superstar was up front in the action. Once she figured out how to start the puzzle, the other girls slowly brushed her aside and finished the game. After the girls finished that puzzle and got the code that opens a lockbox on the wall, I heard one girl saying, "How did everyone figure that out?" at which point one of the girls went back to the puzzle and showed her. No credit was given to Ms. Superstar, who had advanced the group's game by providing all the correct answers.

Things were now down to the wire for the girls. They were out of hints and only had a minute left. All they had to do was get the final code to disarm the nuclear bomb, and they would be victorious. However, no one could figure out the last code. Ms. Superstar ventured into the area where the last code is contained. After a short time, she casually said the final number. Victory! The green light turned on, signaling that they had disarmed the bomb and won the game with seconds to spare. The girls screamed so loud that the people in the lobby could hear them. They ran out of the room, jumping, screaming, and skipping to the lobby in excitement.

I took the group's picture and congratulated the girls on a job well done. After the picture, the girls were talking about their experience to the other teams that had recently finished their own rooms. All the groups at that point had passed, and the atmosphere was electric. The parents were all happy, and everyone was riding an adrenaline high. After the last room got out, I took photos of all the players from each individual room and a group photo consisting of all four groups together and thanked them coming out.

While leaving the business, I heard one of the girls from my room ask another girl "How did we figure some of that stuff out?" to which the other girl replied, "I don't know," laughing as she walked out the front door. I know how they had won, and I wish I had been quicker on my feet to tell the group why they had escaped: one of the girls in the room had discovered all of the answers. I remember four different instances throughout the game in which Ms. Superstar, alone, produced the answer that the group was looking for. On all four occasions not one person acknowledged that it was her who had figured out the puzzle. She was never included in the group yet was essential to its success. Without her the final number to disarm the bomb would not have been discovered. Without her the game would have been lost and Dayton would have been evaporated in a huge mushroom cloud; yet, no one noticed.

This book isn't about me giving advice on or telling someone what they should do in life but rather an observation of what I have seen watching more than 1,500 escape rooms. However, after that game I couldn't help but wonder how often we don't recognize the people in our life, whether at work or at home, who have the answers and don't get any recognition for it. Sometimes superstars aren't in front of us, but rather they are behind us. It's up to us to discover whom they are and give them credit and recognition.

OBSERVATION 20

Give credit when credit is due.

CHAPTER TWENTY-ONE

How Women Play Escape Rooms

"She believed she could; so, she did."

—UNKNOWN ARTIST—

I might take some flak for these chapters discussing men and women, and I'm well prepared for that. My goal is to not interject my opinion or show bias in any way. The entire purpose of this book is to simply tell people what I have observed with men and women and the multitudes of different players that have come through my business. Sometimes I hardly notice any patterns, but other times the distinctions can be plain as day. We will start this journey discussing how women play escape rooms.

The first couple of months of watching escape games I hardly noticed any differences in the way women and men interacted with their own gender or with the opposite sex. Things, such as words used by the escape room players, were much easier to notice and observe than the subtle actions of the individual genders. Maybe I never cared to notice or didn't know what I was looking or listening for. However, after these first couple of months, patterns started to become impossible to ignore. There were clearly differences between how women and men interacted with their own gender and the other sex, and once you saw them, you couldn't help but notice them in every game. The first time something stuck out to me was when I was watching a group of women playing the Bank Vault room.

I had a group of women come in to play the Bank Vault as a team building exercise one day. None of the women had ever played an escape game before, and they all were very excited to attempt a robbery of our bank room. I got a chance to talk to most of the group members several minutes prior to putting them in the room. The start of the game had been delayed because the group was waiting on someone who was running late (I won't go there). The women were probing me for information on how to win the room and for any additional clues that could help them escape the Bank Vault. They asked me if women were better than men at playing escape rooms. What a tricky question that was. I told them that both genders had different approaches to the game and that one gender wasn't better than the other. They kind of teased me and didn't accept my politically correct answer. They continued to press and probe me to get my opinion on who was better. Trying to remain neutral, I told them just one thing I noticed a couple days prior with a group of all women. I explained it like this. When there are only women in a group, the tendency is for all the women in the room to bunch together to look at the same thing. This is true even if they know a divide and conquer approach is best. It appears having a support system is important. Again, I am not anything close to an expert on the differences between the genders; however, I have noticed that on most occasions in which the escape room consists only of women, they tend to form groups and focus on one thing at a time as one unit. I told the group waiting in the lobby this observation and stressed to them that in this room divide and conquer is the best strategy. Just then, the final group member arrived, and we were ready to start. I went over the rules and brought the group into the Bank Vault.

After five minutes in the room, the group had tripped the alarm. All seven of the women hovered around the alarm trying to figure out a way to shut it off. For several minutes the group didn't move from the alarm. Some of the group members were looking at the alarm not even trying to solve the annoying beeping. Eventually they turned off the alarm, and the group dispersed. A couple of minutes later a woman found something in the room that needed to be opened. She told the assembly of players that she had discovered an object, and they all dropped what they were doing to hover around the newly acquired item. For at least 30 seconds the entire room stared and huddled around this object. Knowing they were stuck, the women asked for a hint, figured out how to open said object, and moved forward in the game.

Later in the experience, a woman found a key near the desk in the room. She proudly proclaimed that she located another key, at which point everyone in the room stopped what she was doing and followed the woman around the room as she looked for a matching lock for this newly found tool. The key went to one of the lockers. As the key turned, everyone watched with excitement to see what was in the locker. Throughout the game this pattern of grouping together occurred regularly, which didn't necessarily hurt the group but also didn't help it either. The group ended up beating the room with more than five minutes left. Afterward, I spoke to the woman with whom I'd had the earlier conversation about women grouping together, and I asked her if she noticed that her teammates had bunched together on several occasions. She responded by telling me that they had not grouped together once in the room. She didn't even notice that they assembled six times throughout the game. I did, though, and from then on, I wouldn't be able to not notice it when watching all subsequent groups consisting of women only.

Another difference I've observed with women is their willingness to be supportive of and encouraging toward each other. Although this reassurance doesn't always happen, it occurs often enough to notice. A group consisting only of women, with no males in the room, would often say things like "Good job," "Way to go," "You're the best," "I'm glad you're doing this game with us," and several other motivating phrases. If someone solved a puzzle or clue in an escape room with all women, the rest of the women, on average, would cheer, applaud, high five, or even hug! A general sense of excitement and accomplishment was usually in order after completing a step in the process to finish a room. On many occasions I have seen a group of women complete the second to last puzzle in the room and virtually stop playing the game due to everyone's excitement and complimentary nature. My favorite example of this comes from another group of women playing the Bank Vault on separate occasion.

This team was average in most regards, and the game progressed at a standard rate of play. The end of the game was upon them, and all they needed to do was get the big moneybag unlocked from the security cabinet, load the loot, and escape the room. There was a minute left in the game, and even I was starting to feel the pressure. Finally, the group figured out the code to unlock the big moneybag. Cheers and high fives all around! The group members were congratulating themselves, as they now had the moneybag in hand. The problem was that they still needed to load the bag and escape the room before the time ran out! I quickly got on the microphone to remind them to load the loot and escape! Chaos ensued as the individuals rapidly tossed the gold, silver, diamonds, and other loot into the bag. People were running into each other during the pandemonium. They escaped the room with two seconds to spare! If I didn't get on the microphone to put a fire under their butts, they would have all been jailed. This same scenario and behavior have occurred several times and in nearly all of the six rooms that we offer. It's always entertaining to watch a group, especially if it celebrates before winning the game!

This grouping behavior occurs more commonly than not when it comes to groups with all women in them. An interesting thing happens though when you add just one man to an all-women assembly. The behavior of clustering and cheering each other on, that is so typical in all women groups, drastically is reduced. The noticeable encouragement and verbal praising of each other can, on some occasions, become non-existent when a male is introduced to the room. Again, I am not a scientist, psychologist, or anything of the sort. I am an entrepreneur that is simply informing you what I have observed watching more than 1,500 escape room experiences.

In a group of six women it is common to see the women praise each other and bunch together to see what is going on. Throw a male into a crew of six women and the entire atmosphere changes. When the male is introduced you might see smaller groups of two, sometimes three, women group together instead of the entire collection. These women, in the new setting with a male in the room, may still praise or be encouraging to each other, but the volume is always reduced. In not one single experience that I have watched, when at least one male is in the room, has the group been as audible as I have seen previous groups that consisted of all women. I understand this may sound ridiculous, and if you told me this two years ago, I probably wouldn't have believed you; however, like I said, this is what I have observed from watching more than 1,500 escape rooms in the past two years.

OBSERVATION 21

Be supportive and empower one another.

CHAPTER TWENTY-TWO

How Men Play Escape Rooms

"Nearly all men can stand adversity,
but if you want to test a man's character,
give him power."

−ABRAHAM LINCOLN−

I've seen a lot of different ways that people communicate with one another while playing escape games. Some people are quiet and methodical, while others are loud and chaotic. One of the most interesting forms of communication came one day when two young couples came to play the Outbreak. Sometimes I have extra time before a game begins and can talk to the customers prior to the start of their experience. I enjoy this for several reasons. One, I get a chance to ask where they heard about us, which is vital information for my business and marketing efforts. Two, I get to hear a little bit about them, their experience with escape rooms, where they are from, and all sorts of different subjects.

I was chatting with two young couples before starting their game and discovered that they love playing escape rooms and have done quite a few. They were excited about the challenge of playing our second hardest room, which had only a 15 percent escape rate, and seemed to be more than confident that they would beat the room. I also discovered that the two men in the group were second lieutenants in the United States Air Force. This didn't surprise me too much given our location was about three miles away from a very large air force base. The four individuals were ready to play the game, and so I took them to the outside of the Outbreak laboratory to go over the rules. Being that they were very experienced with escape rooms, I didn't give them any small hints in the beginning or bonus hints before putting them inside the room. I went over the instructions and started the 60-minute timer.

This group was flying through the puzzles and got into the second room in almost record time. The players were not getting held up on anything. They were on pace to get out of the room with 30 minutes left in the game, a time unthinkable for the Outbreak. A group of expert escape room artists had beaten the Outbreak earlier in the year with around 25 minutes left, but no other groups have come close to that in all the time we've had our Outbreak room. Communication among all four individuals couldn't have been better. They were direct, concise, and all four of them were on the same page. Then, something stimulating happened when they got to the last conundrum of the room. This puzzle of the Outbreak is the hardest game in any of our rooms, especially one specific part of the puzzle that most people get stuck on. It is common for people to not understand what to do on this part of the puzzle and get frustrated, sometimes with each other more than the puzzle itself. This group of four superstars was no different.

Upon arriving at the final piece of the last puzzle in the game, the group got stuck. Confusion had taken over for the only time in the very short period that the group had spent in the room. Then something almost scary happened. The two guys started getting very loud and began yelling at each other. The women in the room slowly backed up and got out of the way from the guys who were getting brasher and louder. It appears one of the lieutenants was putting his finger in the other lieutenant's chest as he was yelling his explanation of the puzzle. At this point, I was out of my chair about to leave the game master room to arbitrate. This option of intervening didn't sound that fun to me. I was dreading going in there. One of the of two guys was probably 6'4" and weighing 225 pounds or more. I'm not a tiny guy, but stepping in the middle of these two military men shouting at each other was not something I had particularly wanted to do on my Wednesday night! Just as I was about to go into the room and break things up, one of the guys shouted, "You're right," and the other guy shouted back "Ok then." They asked me if it was the right code, and the two girls that had left the room came back in. Everything was back to normal.

They finished the game with more than 22 minutes to spare. After the experience ended, I congratulated them and informed them that they were seconds away from breaking a record for the room. I took their picture, and they were all happy. I mentioned that things got a little heated in the room, and all four of them laughed. One of the girls said, "We have personal goals for ourselves when it comes to winning escape rooms, and sometimes that's just how they talk to each other." They all smiled, joked, congratulated one other, and then left my business.

For the two guys in the room, this form of communication with each other was normal. The girls didn't seem to mind, and the lieutenants appeared to be very close friends. I have never seen two women yelling at each other in that manner, at least not in an escape room. Maybe a disagreement occurs from time to time, but shouting and finger-pointing like that in an escape room? Not a chance. The communication process of the two men worked extremely well for them; although, I don't recommend it. The two couples came back months afterwards to play another game, for which they very nearly set the record again. Thankfully, they did it this time without any yelling.

One theme I commonly see with men is their physically dominating behavior. Often, I will see men physically remove something out of a woman or child's hand or push them out of the way to look at a clue. This behavior is more common if there is someone smaller in size in the room with them as opposed to someone of similar or larger proportion. If the room consists of all men, then you will almost never see a smaller man ripping something out of a bigger man's hand.

A classic example of this is when I watched a family play Area D one weekend. From the beginning of the game the dad of the group was being obnoxious talking over everyone and barking orders like he had all the answers. We'll call him Mr. Macho. All throughout the game Mr. Macho would move his kids and wife out of the way when he wanted to look at something. He would constantly take the different puzzles and clues out of everyone's hands for no reason and sometimes would just set it back down as though he was simply doing it to show that he's the boss. Imagine trying to solve a puzzle and someone continuously interrupting you. It's like having Peter Griffin from Family guy in an escape room with you. The worst part about watching Mr. Macho and his family play the escape room was the fact that he would get angry and loud if someone pushed back a little bit. Of course, he didn't contribute at all to the success of the game, and everything that came out of his mouth was wrong. But hey, did you expect any different?

The group ended up getting about halfway through the game before the bomb turned their bodies to ash. Every time the family made progress; the aggressive nature of Mr. Macho would get them off track. Aggression and machismo may be useful in the WWE or UFC, but if you want to win an escape room, leave that king of the jungle attitude at home. Of course, not all men act in this domineering manner. I have watched several games in which the male in the room worked with everyone in an equal and fair fashion.

OBSERVATION 22

Play on your strengths,
but also know your weaknesses.

CHAPTER TWENTY-THREE

The Person Who Knows Everything

"The dumbest people I know are those who know it all."
—MALCOLM FORBES—

A gentleman came into our escape room and booked the Vault for himself and two of his friends, one of which was with him and the other that was on the way. We'll call this gentleman Mr. Lead Me Not. While waiting for the third player to arrive, I got a chance to speak with the players in the lobby. We started talking about their past experiences in escape rooms. Mr. Lead Me Not has played at our location and at other escape room businesses in Ohio. The conversation with Mr. Lead Me Not led to him talking about one of the games that he and his friends played and lost about a month ago at a different business. He was bummed they had lost and told me that they were very close to winning. He then started blaming his friend, who was waiting in the lobby with him, for their loss. "We wouldn't have failed if it wasn't for you," Mr. Lead Me Not said. The next couple of minutes comprised of this man telling me that he was the leader of the group and how, without him, his friends wouldn't have gotten anywhere in any of the rooms they've played. I explained to them that our escape rooms are hard for just two people and that I was glad they had a third person coming. Mr. Lead Me Not then blurted out "Oh, our friend coming is an idiot and won't be helping us out." This pretty much set the tone for one of the most painful hours I have ever had to endure at the Great Escape Game.

When the final group member arrived, I brought them to the room and started explaining the rules. While I was going over the instructions, Mr. Lead Me Not wanted me to stop because he was ready to play and didn't need to be bothered by all this stuff. "I've got this," he proclaimed. I put the three stooges in the room, prepared for the worst, and wasn't disappointed.

All throughout the game Mr. Lead Me Not was bossing the other two group members around. He would say things like, "That's not how you do it" or "why would you do that?" The criticism never seemed to end. I don't know how these two individuals stayed in the room with him. Mr. Lead Me Not was wrong on virtually everything. From the simplest of puzzles to the more complex, he didn't come close to having a correct answer on anything. Somehow, the group managed to progress through the room and got close to the end.

The group members figured out the combination to the big safe in the room, and all they had to do was open it and then accomplish a couple small things after that to win. On the big safe there are instructions regarding how to open it. The instructions are on a dry-erase board, and the players in the game can write down the numbers on the corresponding lines that tell them how to work the turn dial. Who do you suppose tried to open the safe? You guessed it, Mr. Lead Me Not himself. With five minutes left in the game they had more than enough time to win. There was only one problem. Mr. Lead Me Not couldn't get the safe open. Loudly, he proclaimed that the safe doesn't open and that they have the wrong numbers to open it. I came over the microphone and confirmed that the digits they had were indeed correct. They had the numbers right; they just needed to slow down and follow the instructions.

I watched Mr. Lead Me Not closely and noticed that he was turning the dial the wrong way on the first combination. I came back over the microphone and told him to turn the dial counterclockwise, or left, four times, landing on the first digit the fourth time they saw it. Mr. Lead Me Not proclaimed that's what he did, and that the problem was the safe not him. He tried again, and at this point I was walking him through every step. The third combination needed to be turned counterclockwise, or left, yet he turned it clockwise. I told him that he needed to turn the dial counterclockwise for the third digit. Once again, he informed me that he did it right and that it just won't open. Four minutes passed quickly, and the team, if you wanted to call it that, was down to the last minute.

By this time the group wouldn't be able to pass. I wanted to see the players at least open the safe as this may give them the feeling of accomplishment. I was on the microphone, walking them through every turn of the dial and again Mr. Lead Me Not wouldn't listen to me and turned the dial the wrong way on one of the digits. Busted! The time was up, and everyone was under arrest. I walked into the room, and Mr. Lead Me Not stated very loudly, "It's impossible to open this safe!" Although this guy was one of a kind, I still didn't want him or the group to leave my business dissatisfied. I asked them to try to open the safe one more time with me right next to them, instructing while they attempted to open it. The first turn of the dial: success. A second and a third turn went according to plan. Now all they had to do was turn the dial clockwise to the final number, and the safe would open. I told Mr. Lead Me Not to turn the dial to the right, landing on the final number the first time he saw it. During what seemed like a bad dream, he turned the dial to the left instead of the right. Even as I was telling him he was doing it wrong; he pushed through and turned the dial left until it landed on the final number. The safe didn't open and Mr. Lead Me Not was furious. I offered to open the safe for the group, but he refused, much to the disappointment of the other players.

They left the room, and we got their picture in the lobby. As they were leaving, Mr. Lead Me Not was telling me how the safe was impossible to open and then proceeded to blame his teammates for not doing better before they got to the that point in the game. I genuinely felt sorry for the others in the group as they left.

If there ever was an example of what a leader was not, this guy was it. Mr. Lead Me Not never listened. Not to me, or his friends, or anyone else for that matter. He never admitted that he didn't know what he was doing, and he refused to let anyone else except him work on something that was important. The worst part about Mr. Lead Me Not was the fact that he blamed everyone else for problems the group faced. He was never to blame. Do you know anyone that is like Mr. Lead Me Not? I hope it's not you.

OBSERVATION 23

No one knows everything.

CHAPTER TWENTY-FOUR

The Different Types of Players

*"It takes all kinds to make
the world go 'round."*
−TRENT SHELTON−

Leadership and communication skills are vital elements for a team to successfully beat an escape room. In each escape room experience, there is a range of
different roles that people take on. From team leader to the distractor, everyone finds his or her natural state of leadership, or lack thereof. In the 1,500-plus
games I've watched, I have noticed patterns of different types of people in
escape rooms. The six most common types of people I see are the leaders, the
doers, the distractors, the observers, the thinkers, and the cheerleaders.

The doers are those that, after they understand the task at hand, dive right
into it and immediately start working to finish. Typically, the leader will delegate
the task to the doers and then continue looking at the big picture of the room
and the puzzles in it. Other times the doer will figure out puzzles on his or her
own and will move straight into finishing the task with little direction or input
from others.

You might think that doers are the most common type of people. In my
experience, the maximum numbers of doers in a room at any a given time is
two. Sometimes there are no doers at all, which makes it challenging for
groups to get through puzzles that require time and focus. For example, in
our Outbreak room there is a moment toward the middle of the game in
which players discover some components to a puzzle. A sure-fire way to tell if
someone is a doer is to watch the behavior of the people once they get all the
pieces to this puzzle. The doer will immediately start plugging away at the
game. The game mentioned in the Outbreak is very time consuming and
takes considerable concentration to accomplish. When a doer starts on this

game, he or she often is so focused that he or she doesn't even tell everyone what he or she, the doer, is doing; he or she just starts working on it. If someone asks the doer how it works, the doer may take the time to explain it but won't take his or her attention away from the game.

This behavior is very different from that of the other types of people. Distractors might throw the pieces of the game at each other. Leaders will understand what to do with the game and will often delegate the task to someone else. The cheerleaders will tell the person working on a puzzle how good of a job they are doing. Another example of noticing when someone is a doer can be seen in our Bank Vault.

Throughout most of the hour in the Bank Vault, players find map pieces for a security camera layout. There is a total of 28 pieces, found in no particular order, which makes assembling the map somewhat difficult. One can identify the doer in the room easily when it comes to assembling the puzzle. The doer will stay on the puzzle until he or she gets to a point in which he or she needs more pieces. The only way he or she will break from the puzzle is if he or she hears someone in the room talk about another task that needs to be done. When a duty is at hand and needs to be accomplished, doers are the people you want in the room with you. It is rare when there is not a doer in a room full of people, but when there isn't one, the group can struggle to stay focused or to get through the different puzzles.

The distractors are often hard to detect in a group. This is because they appear to be active throughout the entire game. The only problem is that their liveliness isn't contributing to the success of the group. These individuals might be frequently asking for hints, but they aren't trying to solve anything or, worse, they are harassing players who are.

The most recent group with a noticeable distractor I observed was playing the Tomb. While I was going over the rules, this individual kept cracking jokes and asking questions that weren't related to escape rooms or what they were about to attempt to solve. Normally, this isn't a big deal, and cracking jokes and asking distracting questions before a game doesn't necessarily guarantee a label of "distractor"; however, in this case the disturbances never stopped. Two minutes into the game, the distractor started shouting, asking for a hint with his arms raised in the air. These requests for hints continued throughout the next 15 minutes. You are probably thinking to yourself, what's the big deal? After watching several hundred escape room games you start to notice all the little details in the room. In this case, every time this individual screamed and flailed about, the players working on a game piece or puzzle would look up or take their attention away from what they were working on. This distraction might only be for a second, but when it disrupts someone's thought process, especially in the middle of solving a puzzle, the long-term effect is multiplied significantly.

Every time the doers and leaders look up, the group loses several seconds. I know, I know; you're thinking, "That's it? We're only talking about seconds here?" No, the group loses a lot more than that. It takes a certain amount of time to get the brain ramped up when working on a puzzle. It could take a couple minutes of concentration to get near solving a puzzle, but after that two-second distraction the puzzle-solver's mind reverts to the beginning of the solving process or his or her attention shifts slightly elsewhere. I've seen it dozens of times. An individual is just about to solve a puzzle, and then— Bam! The distractor swoops in! I've witnessed people giving up on a clue and walking away moments before they were about to complete the task, all because of a distractor.

Now I'm not saying that just talking will derail someone who is close to finishing a project. Rather, it's the manner in which it's done. For example, if someone were to come by and ask an individual working on a project what they have finished so far, it can have a positive impact as the person can talk things out loud to themselves or others, which can provide him or her with more clarity on the task at hand. However, when a distractor comes up to someone, takes what they are working on out of that person's hands, moves it to a different spot, and then walks away, this can, and often does, have negative effects. These frequent interruptions by the distractor in the Tomb caused the group, who may have originally done well, to fail miserably.

Leaders are the most important individuals in an escape room. A leader can deliver his or her group to victory or send them to failure. Sometimes, leaders are found in the very spot you'd hope to see them in. One example of leadership comes from a barter the Great Escape Game did with a local restaurant. I traded several escape room tickets with a nearby eatery, enough to bring the entire staff into our escape rooms. I wanted the manager and the owner of the franchise to play, and I would stop in often to their restaurant to try to convince them to join the employees they would send to play. Finally, my persistence prevailed, and I got the owner and the general manager to come and play our Western Saloon room. Both individuals had never done this before, had no clue what to expect, but had high expectations that the experience would be fun. I went over the rules with everyone and started their game.

The group started off very slowly and was struggling to move forward. I convinced the team members to use a hint after 15 minutes of them not doing much to complete the room. After the hint, the group completed the next couple of puzzles on its own. While the team members were searching for clues and trying to figure out the next steps, the owner of the restaurant was going around the room quietly searching every piece of furniture, the walls, and anything else that could be of use. The owner ended up finding a hidden object in the room and calmly told the group what he discovered. Play continued at a normal rate until one of the team members became frustrated and appeared to quit. The owner of the restaurant encouraged her to not give up and then continued his quest to figure things out.

In the last 15 minutes of the game, the owner would discover or figure out every puzzle. He never bragged or gloated, and his demeanor was always calm. It was coming down to the wire, and the game was on the line. You could hear the horses outside as the gang of cowboys got closer and closer to busting through the saloon doors with their guns drawn. The group needed to find the last missing piece that would give them the code to the final box with the deed to the saloon in it. Moving at a methodical pace, the owner found this last item that would give the other players the final code they needed. They grabbed the deed to the saloon, put on their cowboy hats, and escaped with under a minute left in their game. Victory! There was a big sigh of relief from the group. The manager was stressed out (in a good way) and claimed she had no idea that the game would be so hard.

The employees were celebrating their win, and the owner was still cool, calm, and collected. They beat that game because of the owner, but you would never know that by listening to the conversation. The owner congratulated his employees and told them how great of a job they all did. He didn't try to take any credit for the victory even though there was plenty to give to him. After the pictures the owner and manager thanked us and went about their day. Being a leader isn't about taking all the credit and boasting to everyone how great you are. It's about recognizing the power of the team, putting your head down, and doing what needs to be done to support the mission.

Thinkers can often be described as the engineering types. These individuals are always processing every bit of information they receive throughout the hour-long experience. Thinkers can be active in the participation aspect of the puzzles or they can convert into deep thinkers that go far down the rabbit hole in search of an answer. So far down that they can go minutes without being involved in the game, all without even realizing they're disconnected from the room. Since I have a chapter later discussing engineers and the thinker types, I'll move on to bring the conversation to observers and cheerleaders.

Observers are an interesting bunch to watch. I did some observation, myself, one Wednesday afternoon while serving as game master to a group of program managers and engineers from the local air force base who had come to play the Outbreak escape room. This group seemed rather normal, and the group members split into their respective roles almost immediately after the timer begin. After watching the group play for about 15 minutes, I started to notice that one gentleman in the room wasn't speaking, and for the first quarter of the experience he didn't say a word. This isn't to say that this man wasn't involved in the game. To the contrary, he was one of the most active individuals in the room. If anyone opened something, discovered an item, or even talked out loud about a puzzle he or she had found, he was there. Without missing a single detail this gentleman was a part of every piece of the game. When players found a medical bag, he would inspect it. Should a puzzle have a riddle that needed solved, he would read it carefully. There was even a moment in the room when a key was revealed, and urged by his curiosity, the observer grabbed the key to examine it closely. What's out of place about this, you might ask? Well, during all of this participation from this guy, he never said a word. Thirty minutes had gone by, and this guy could probably have drawn the room to scale; yet, not the slightest of sounds came from his mouth.

I watched him very closely for the second half-hour and saw the same results as the first 30 minutes. With seven minutes to go in the game, the players were on the last riddle. They seemed to be stuck, and the moment for which I had waited so patiently had arrived. The guy that didn't say a word for 53 minutes went to the cabinet where the clue was, grabbed the paper that had the pertinent information on it, appeared to be reading it, and then after a very long 30 seconds handed the sheet off to someone else. How frustrating it was for me to watch! Why didn't he say anything? Perhaps he couldn't speak at all. His teammates never gave me the idea that his quietness bothered them. His actions were normal to everyone in the room but me.

They figured out the last puzzle, found the antidote to the deadly virus, and passed the Outbreak. I walked up to the group, which was celebrating in the hallway, and asked the players if they'd had fun. While everyone was telling me how much fun the experience was, I found myself staring at the guy who hadn't said anything. His eyes rolled up and shifted gaze to the top left, giving the impression that he was deep in thought. After what seemed like an eternity, he said, "It was interesting."

I took the group's end-of-the-game photo, and the group members appeared to leave as happy customers. I sat in the lobby pondering what I just saw and experienced. Everyone in the group, including the guy, had had a good time, but for the entire hour he didn't say a word. Not the slightest sound. Nothing. It was the first time I noticed an observer in one of my escape rooms, but it wouldn't be the last. I could have asked this guy about all the puzzles and props in the room, and he probably wouldn't have any problem recalling everything in detail. But observers are just that; they sit back and observe. They aren't dumb or negative in attitude, and they don't necessarily want the group to fail, but their participation and audibility in the rooms is always limited.

The next type of players, which are always my favorite to watch, are the cheerleaders. Leaders lead, doers do, thinkers think, observers observe, distractors distract, and cheerleaders cheer. A classic example of this occurred one day in the Egyptian Tomb. A group of women from a local salon was attempting an escape room for the first time. There were five women total, and each one of them had expressed her concern over her ability to pass the room. I reassured the five women that they were more than capable of passing, read them the rules, and put them inside the Tomb.

The game started off slow, and the women were struggling a little bit to make any progress. I came over the microphone early and gave them the free hint to look closer at one of the rocks in the room because it contained a secret number. One of the women picked up the rock and found the secret code that was written on the bottom. She proclaimed to the group she had found a code. At this point one of the group members, we'll call her Mrs. Delightful, rushed to the individual that found the code and told her "Awesome job!" The group cheered, and play proceeded.

The next time a group member solved a riddle, Mrs. Delightful told her how wonderful she was. Things picked up for the women, and they started gaining steam, until they got stuck on a part of the game that is designed to hold up groups. I came over the microphone and asked if they wanted to use another hint, to which they replied no rather quickly. While Mrs. Delightful and her teammates struggled to find the answers to the next puzzle, she told them that she knew they would get the answers and how smart everyone in the room is. Almost immediately after this emotional pump up, one of the players discovered the secret to the riddle. Mrs. Delightful couldn't hold back and gave the puzzle solver a big hug, telling her how great she was. The individual receiving the hug couldn't hold back and displayed one of the biggest smiles I have or would ever see at the Great Escape Game.

The group of salon employees would pass the Tomb with 60 seconds left. Everyone was ecstatic, and high fives and congratulations went around to everyone. I took the group's picture, sold all of the women t-shirts, and saw them leave as happy customers. It was refreshing to watch such an enthusiast and supporting individual play one of my escape rooms. I went back to reset the Tomb for the next group, and something dawned on me. Mrs. Delightful never solved one puzzle in the 59 minutes that she was inside the Tomb. In fact, I don't recall her even helping to solve any of the parts of the game. But that wasn't her job. She didn't need to be the smartest or the most analytical in the room. Solving puzzles was never on her agenda. She had a much more important role in the experience. Her job was to boost the morale of the team, and she didn't disappoint. Sometimes we lose sight of the importance of that one person who builds us up. A cheerleader may not know how to solve our problems but is never short of supporting us on our journey to find the answers we are looking for.

OBSERVATION 24

A group always knows more than an individual.

CHAPTER TWENTY-FIVE

Making Things Harder Than They Are

*"Don't get too deep; it leads to over thinking,
and over thinking leads to problems that
don't even exist in the first place."*

−JAYSON ENGAY−

It was a rather busy Thursday when a group arrived celebrating a birthday for a 13-year-old. I was busy resetting the room that I had just finished watching and didn't have time to interact with the group. One of my employees that had extra time put them into their room for me. After finishing my reset, I went back to the game master room to watch the birthday party group. The group had been in the room for about two minutes when I started watching. Since I hadn't put the players in the room, I wasn't sure if any of them had tried an escape room before. I always want to know the history and, more importantly, the mindset of the group prior to the game, as this will affect how I perform my duties as a game master.

The group was struggling badly from the beginning, and I found myself helping the players early on. One of the reasons they were doing so poorly was the fact that when they found something in the room, they would move it to the opposite side of the room where they had discovered it. The Outbreak is one of the hardest rooms we have, but it is achievable. Throughout the entire game you will find a clue that needs another part to complete it. In every single puzzle and clue in the Outbreak, except one, the second part to the puzzle is right next to the first part. When I say right next to, I mean it's usually less than a foot away from the answer or the tool needing to be used to find the solution.

In the starting room, one of the first things you'll discover is a red medical bag. The answer to opening the red medical bag is found right next to where players find the bag, yet, often, people will take the bag to the next room and then leave it on the countertop opposite of where it needs to be. This group was no exception. With every different clue in the game the group would move the part of the puzzle it had found as far away from the solution as possible. For example, toward the beginning of the game players discover an autopsy card in the medical body bag and on the autopsy card are four body parts written in red. On the wall next to the body bag and autopsy report is a huge poster of the muscular structure of a human. Each muscle, or body part, has a corresponding number on the poster. All you need to do is grab the report, look at the body parts written in red, then turn toward the poster and find the numbers on the poster that correspond to the body parts written on the autopsy card. This group did the opposite of that and carried the autopsy report into the next room. The group members then placed the report face down in a binder holder on the wall! After a couple minutes they had forgotten that they had even discovered the autopsy report in the first place. The group had to use a hint to get them past that stage in the game.

Toward the middle of the experience the players discover a second red medical bag. This bag contains multiple pieces of a puzzle. Without being told what the puzzle is, the players need to use something on the desk a foot away from where they discovered the second red medical bag. Instead of using the tools right in front of them, the group took the second red medical bag and its contents and moved them to the other room far away from where the bag needed to be. After much wasted time the players brought the bag back into the room, and the group solved the puzzle.

It was getting close to the end of the game, and things weren't looking too hot for the group. At this point I had been generous with the clues. I could tell they wanted to win; so, I didn't mind giving an extra hint or two. Toward the end, in the second room the group had opened a drawer that would lead it to the last two puzzles in the game. In that drawer, there is a binder labeled TESTING MATERIALS in rather large font and six containers of colored sand, each labeled testing material. On the countertop directly above where they opened the desk drawer with the binder and sand in it is a scale that is labeled TESTING MATERIAL WEIGHT STATION. If you were to open a drawer with a binder that says testing material, containers that say testing materials, all under a scale that says testing material weight station, wouldn't you think that those items are related in some manner? This group didn't think in that way. In fact, more than half the groups I've watched don't think the three items go together. Instead a couple of the girls grabbed the sand containers, while another took the binder. Where did the sand and binder end up? You guessed it: they ended up in the other room far away from where it needed to be. Why did this happen? We aren't trying to deceive anyone in our rooms. Well, maybe we are a little bit but not to the extreme that it's impossible to figure out or, worse, frustrating to the players. As I mentioned, we often put the first part of a puzzle right next to the answer or near the area in which they need to input a code.

The group ended up failing the room. Unfortunately, the group made things harder than they needed to be. On almost every hurdle along the way the players had made their lives more difficult by overcomplicating things and not looking right in front of them. Sometimes in life we do the same. We think the answer can't be right in front of us, and we move things away from the solution when we don't have to.

In the Outbreak, we purposely put the answers to the different puzzles right next to the clues to allow one person to discover a clue and find the solution by him or herself. Although it rarely happens this way, it can be done. The Area D room is like the Outbreak in the fact that the clues and puzzles are in the same proximity. However, in Area D most of the clues are just far enough away that it wouldn't be as efficient if just one person attempted to accomplish things by him or herself. In fact, we built the room specifically to force people to have to communicate with one another to progress through the game. In this room, there are more games that require two or more people to complete the puzzles than any of our other five rooms. This is the main reason why Area D is the hardest room we have at the Great Escape.

One time, I was watching a room in which the players worked for a national communication and leadership business. They were in town for work and had always wanted to try an escape game. Working in the field of communication gave them an edge in the game—or so they thought; so, they decided they would start off with the hardest room first, regardless of its daunting 10 percent escape rate. Smart, right? I'm an optimist and thought that they could beat the room and emerge victorious from our most difficult challenges, even if they hadn't done a room before. Oh boy, was I wrong. Right from the start of the game the group struggled.

As I've mentioned in previous chapters, you and your group start Area D by being handcuffed to the wall at different locations throughout the room, making the discovery of the key a bit trickier than if you were all together in one spot. Sometimes, during the start of Area D someone takes over and starts telling everyone in the room where the key must be. Surely a group of leadership and communication experts wouldn't have a know-it-all in the group, right? Wrong. The person who was closest to the key was telling everyone else where the key must be located. "Look over there. How about in the drawer? It must be over by you." After struggling for five minutes I gave them a freebie to get them un-cuffed.

One of the first puzzles in the game requires someone to listen to a message, hear a secret code, and then relay that message to someone nearby who inputs that code into a game prop. Sound simple? Sometimes it is easy for a group to accomplish this. With this group, however, it was far from simple. There was a huge problem with communication between the individual listening to the code and the person writing it down. The listener would give wrong information, and the person writing this wrong information down would miss some of the things the listener was saying. What this group had was an incoherent message not being written down properly and then being translated into a wrong code. After five minutes, I couldn't take it anymore and offered to help, which they gladly accepted.

Later on, there is a game that requires two individuals to move sliding drawers up and down to get a series of numbers. The game is very difficult to start, but once you figure out how to move the drawers in the correct order it becomes rather straightforward. Most groups struggle with the start of this puzzle and some even burn a hint on it. I thought this group would try to figure it out, talk it over when they ran into any difficulties, and then find a solution. What ended up happening was that the group members started arguing with one another about how to start the game. After a brief tussle, one of the group members took over and did it his way.

During this game, I will ask the player or players to say the numbers he, she, or they get out loud as they discover them so that I can make sure they are on the right track. The first number he gave me was wrong and I told him so. This is a group of leadership professionals playing this game. When one of them finds out that he or she is wrong I would expect him or her to step aside, admit to his or her lack of knowledge on the subject matter, and ask for help. That's what happened, right? Right? Not a chance. The individual who took control of the sliding drawer game proceeded to tell everyone else in the group that this was his game and that he knew exactly what he was doing. The problem was that he had no clue what he was doing. Another struggle began until I came over the microphone to help the group. The players finally solved the sliding drawer game and continued trudging through the nuclear room.

Toward the end of Area D there is another part that requires multiple people get involved. Someone needs to relay what he or she sees on the screen in a closet to someone else in the room, while yet another person writes down the letters or numbers that are being found. Typically, the person looking for the objects on the screen will shout out the number or letter he or she has found to another team member who is writing. The process sounds complicated, but it is not so difficult.

This puzzle should have been a breeze for this group. Upon discovering the tablet on the wall in the closet, instead of shouting out what he needed the other players in the room to start looking for, this individual left the closet and tried to find the object himself. This is never a good idea because it takes too much time to do alone, and there are multiple parts to it that make it hard to remember by oneself. Finally, someone in the group asked this individual what he was doing, at which point everyone in the group started working on it together. What should have been a simple search and discover turned into frustration, as miscommunications associated with the objects being searched for arose. One of the members would shout out what he or she needed to find while another member wrongly transcribed the information on the dry-erase board. This code was wrong, and they had already switched the order of the two codes they had previously tried to input. It was chaotic, but the players needed this code for a safe that would lock them out if they tried to input combinations too many times. I had to assist. I got on the microphone and walked them through the puzzle, starting from the beginning.

The time had now run out, and a nuclear bomb would blow them up. It was a complete breakdown in communication that cost them the game. At no point in the game was good teamwork involved. The egos in the room took over, and things that were easy and right in front of them became difficult. The group members were disappointed in themselves but not as disappointed as I feel they should have been, seeing as they were professionals in the communication and leadership industry. It isn't the fact that something is difficult to figure out in one of our rooms. There isn't that much trickery or even distance between the answers and the clues. Often, it is the egos that get in the way of success. It can be hard to admit when you don't know something, but when you put your pride aside and work with your team, you will find that the answers can be right in front of you.

OBSERVATION 25

Try not to make things harder than they need to be.

CHAPTER TWENTY-SIX

How Words Can Impact Morale

"Words can inspire, and words can destroy. Choose yours well."

—ROBIN SHARMA—

"That's what I told you! Why don't you listen?!" a father said harshly to one of his daughters. Another daughter chimed in telling her dad, "You are so mean and unhelpful." The father responded by saying, "Oh, why don't you mind your own business?" in a rude and demeaning tone. Instantly the dynamic in the room changed. At that point in the experience, the group had 20 minutes to go and was on pace to potentially win the second hardest room we had. Frustrated, one of the daughters sat down in the room and remained there for the rest of the game. She was done and did not want to continue trying to solve puzzles or to help the group win the game. Or maybe she did want to keep playing, but the words used by her father turned off any remaining motivation she might have had left. The father in this group didn't seem phased by it and went on playing.

The group needed the last number of the final game in the room as the big clock on the television struck zero. Game over. The family had failed the room and died of the deadly virus. Afterward, we got a picture of the group in our lobby. There was tension in the air, which made the conversations in the room awkward, and the tension followed the group as it left our facility. There isn't a doubt in my mind that those few sentences between the dad and his kids had a negative impact on the performance of the group. A couple weeks after this family with the rude father had attempted the Outbreak, another family of similar demographics came in to try its luck playing the Tomb. This time the atmosphere was a little different.

This family had two daughters about the same age as the daughters in the Outbreak example above. There are a lot of things to open in the Egyptian

Tomb room, and some of the puzzles are unorthodox and hard to figure out. There isn't any technology in the room, and we focus on RFID switches and magnets to strategically open props. The group started off slow because no one in the group had ever done an escape room before. It wasn't long until the group was running on all cylinders and performing like a well-connected unit. The change in speed happened due to the choice of the words the father decided to use while playing the game.

There was a moment when one of the daughters was sure she had the correct item to unlock something on the wall but was wrong in her assumption. The item she had discovered did open something in the room, but it didn't unlock what she was hoping for. The girl was bummed and looked sort of defeated. That would have been her first contribution to the room, and I could tell she wanted to do her part to help her family win. Her father, realizing his daughter was bummed, turned to her and said, "That won't work on there, but awesome idea! Don't give up and keep trying!" The daughter was disappointed that it didn't work out how she had wanted, but her disappointment quickly morphed into an optimistic energy upon hearing her father's words. His words were positive and uplifting. Mistakes were okay in this family.

This became more evident about 20 minutes later when the other daughter was holding two items that need to go together to get a code. The team had asked me to use one of its hints, and so I told the players to put together the two objects that were in the girl's hand to see a hidden message. The daughter was somewhat disappointed that she had both pieces in her hands and couldn't see the connection. Looking down at the ground the daughter said she was so stupid out loud. Her father chimed in immediately and said "No you aren't. You tried, and things didn't work out the way you wanted. That is how we grow." That is power right there. At that point I turned up the volume in the room and started paying closer attention.

Looking back, I should have gotten his name because I'm sure he worked for some sort of leadership seminar. Or maybe he didn't, but the expression on his daughter's face after she had received his advice was nearly impossible to forget. She instantaneously smiled. He put his arm around her and his other daughter as the mother opened the next box in the game. There was a sincere sense of security in that smile. Her dad was on her side. He was a champion to her—someone who would hold her responsible yet support her. There wasn't any animosity whatsoever in that family. Communication wasn't perfect, but it didn't have to be. The family members were a unit with one mission: find the treasure of the pharaoh and escape from the curse! They did just that and with 10 minutes to spare.

After they won the game, they all began high fiving one another. The other daughter was so excited and shouted, "We won!" as she stretched her arms high into the air. We all went to the lobby, and I took their picture as they held up the sign that showed the time in which they'd beat the room. I can still feel the energy from the family long after it left. Those words of encouragement from the father will stay not only with his daughter for a long time but with me as well. Positive and inspiring words can change our lives and, in this case, can help us rob an Egyptian pharaoh.

However, it's not always flowers and roses at the Great Escape Game. About a week-and-a-half after the family with the nice and uplifting father came through, a father with a different attitude decided to come in with his family to play the same room, the Egyptian Tomb. The ages of the kids were about the same as the family with the uplifting father. The only difference was that there was a boy and a girl instead of two girls. Before the game began the dad started to complain about being trapped inside a room, referencing his claustrophobia. I completely understand his concern. Who would want to be locked in a small confined space with the possibility of getting stuck? I reassured him and mentioned the room was a very large open space. He didn't really reply directly to me, but rather he turned his head and said, "Why am I am doing this?" in a not-so-pleasant tone. Around the same time, his son was showing concern by asking me if it was scary. As I was replying to the youngster to tell him there is nothing frightening about any of our rooms, his dad passive-aggressively told his son, "You'll be alright."

This was going to be a long game to watch. All throughout the game the father criticized his kids. These children didn't behave like normal kids their age. They had hesitation in their actions and weren't as curious as other youngsters. At one point, late in the game, the son tried to open a box but was unable to. The kid got upset and started to cry. Without missing a beat, the father snarled at his son and told him, "Quit crying, only losers let their emotions take over." Yep, the father of a young boy told him that crying is for losers. There was a loser in the room all right, but it wasn't the young boy.

The entire team dynamic was awful from the start of the room. There was a complete lack of communication within the group as the father continued his emotional reign of terror. At one point toward the middle of the game he snatched a magnet from his daughter's hand and proclaimed that she had no idea what it went to. Granted, the little girl didn't have any awareness what the magnet went to, but the father didn't either. His actions and words did nothing but tear down his wife and kids. They failed the room miserably.

After the game ended, I walked into the room. The father didn't say anything to his family. He didn't offer any words of encouragement, any "Good jobs," or any suggestions that maybe next time they'll do better. In fact, he wouldn't even look at his kids. He rushed out of the room, leaving everyone behind. In the entire one-and-a-half hours I experienced with this individual, not one second of it was pleasant. His words did not improve his family's ability to win the game but rather had the opposite effect. I wonder what the other family members thought after they lost. Did they blame their failure on themselves? Would they be less encouraged to try a similar experience in the future? The words this guy chose to use, and not use, during the game had a major impact on the result of the experience as well as on the morale of the other players. No amount of money can buy back the spoken word. How often do we think about the words that we use? Do the things we say daily lift people up or bring them down?

OBSERVATION 26

Pay close attention to the words you use.

CHAPTER TWENTY-SEVEN

Fortune Favors the Bold

"Every chance taken is another chance to win."
−ANONYMOUS−

It was the first week of September, and I received a call from a nervous-sounding kid looking for some help with an idea. The young man wanted to play one of our rooms and use the experience to ask a girl to go with him to the homecoming dance at one of the local high schools. What a fun idea! Of course, I was willing to help. The high school kid (we'll call him Mr. Hopeful) and I talked for a couple of minutes about how we would accomplish this goal. He didn't have much detail of how he wanted to do it, but the idea to ask her to the dance at an escape room in general was firmly in his head. They had played a couple of escape rooms together, and he mentioned that she loved them. We discussed the different rooms and tried to figure out which experience would offer the best chance of getting her to say yes to going to the dance with him. We concluded that the perfect room to make the move was the Egyptian Tomb.

In this experience, you and your group of Tomb raiders have been hired to retrieve the riches of the Egyptian pharaoh. After you enter the Tomb, the door slams behind you, and because of the powers of the pharaoh, a curse has come upon you and your fellow band of grave robbers. There was a previous group of Tomb raiders that was sent in weeks ago by the company that hired you, but no one has heard from the previous tomb raiders. As you enter the Tomb, you discover their remains. The only way to escape the curse is to get the treasures of the pharaoh and find a way to remove his curse. You have one hour to find the riches and escape or endure the same fate as the Tomb raider group before you!

The reason we selected the Egyptian Tomb for Mr. Hopeful's plan is because at the end of the game, after you have found the treasure, you need to translate hieroglyphics to remove the curse. Throughout the experience, players gather blocks that have symbols on one side and a letter on the other side showing what that character translates into. At the end of the game, all the blocks in the room are found and placed on multiple shelves on the wall. The last thing players in the Tomb need to do is translate a piece of papyrus paper from the recently opened sarcophagus. The idea we came up with was to change the symbols on the paper so that when it was translated it would say, "Will you go to homecoming with me?"

Mr. Hopeful hadn't yet figured out the exact time and date of when he and his friends could all come to the Great Escape and attempt to get a date to the dance. I told him to call back when he knew the date that everyone could come in and play. A few days later, Mr. Hopeful's group booked The Tomb and was set to play on a Saturday night. I changed the end of the game papyrus paper to read "Will you go to homecoming with me?" I wanted this to work so badly for the young man that I made sure I was working that Saturday so that I could be his group's game master. The big day came around, and I felt like I was more excited than he was. Ironically enough, everyone arrived early except for the girl that Mr. Hopeful was to ask out. The entire group was in on it and knew the plan to ask the girl to the dance at the end of the game. The girl finally made it to Great Escape, and we were off to the Tomb! I was expecting the group to be awkward with such a big secret, but surprisingly all of them kept their cool. I got them inside the Tomb and started their game. I wanted to make the game close, but I had to pass this group or else the whole surprise would be ruined.

Throughout the game, Mr. Hopeful played it cool. He had to be nervous. Heck, I was nervous! I provided the group members with one more hint than I usually do so that they could get to the end with a little under five minutes to play. It was getting close to judgment time.

The ending of the Tomb is the quickest of all six of our rooms, as trap doors start opening rapidly and everything gets exciting quickly. With a final lever activated, the sarcophagus started opening. Everyone was a little hesitant to grab the thousand-year-old paper that was resting on the mummy within. In a stroke of luck, the girl grabbed the script that needed to be transcribed. The group knew they had to translate the symbols on the paper and speedily got to work on doing so. I left the game master room and was waiting outside the

Tomb. I was listening outside of the room for the group to finish translating the paper. My heart was racing; so, I'm sure Mr. Hopeful's was as well. It seemed like I was waiting in the hallway for an eternity. It was like a dramatic scene in a movie. Every second seemed like hours until I heard the room get quiet. I leaned in and then heard some awws. I walked in the room, and everyone had smiles ear to ear. She said yes! The girl was blushing, but she seemed happy. I was ecstatic for Mr. Hopeful. I brought the lovebirds to the lobby, and I took the end-of-game picture. The smiles in those pictures said it all. It was an awesome experience, and I'm glad I could be a part of it. Mr. Hopeful took a chance on love. He could have crashed and burned, but he didn't. Fortune favors the bold. On that Saturday, Mr. Hopeful went from dateless to getting himself a plus-one to homecoming in the most epic of ways.

OBSERVATION 27

There is no failure, only learning.

WILL THEY ESCAPE?

CHAPTER TWENTY-EIGHT

Beware of the Red Herring

"Work is hard. Distractions are plentiful. And time is short."
—ADAM HOCHSCHILD—

When you walk into one of our escape rooms for the first time it can be a little overwhelming. Before you enter an escape room you have no idea what to expect. We don't allow anyone to know what's inside each experience for two main reasons. First, we don't want to accidently give away any clues that might help someone know how beat it before even entering. Secondly, we want it to be exciting and mysterious to enter a themed room, especially if you don't know what to expect. There's a certain buildup that happens prior to walking into an escape room. Your blood is already pumping with excitement, as you know that you only have one hour to complete the experience. If we were to show a room prior to going inside, it would create some familiarity within your mind, which may reduce some of the anxiety that makes the experience exciting.

At the Great Escape Game, we go over all the rules outside of the room, leaving nothing to discuss once inside. After we are done with the instructions, we bring the group in and start the game's introduction video. Once you walk into the room, you are visually over-stimulated by dozens of objects, decorations, and audio effects that hit you all at once. When the game video is finished, the timer starts automatically. The adrenaline rush kicks in, and everyone scatters about the room frantically looking for the first puzzle or clue.

All of the items in our six experiences are related to the overarching theme of the individual room in which it is found. My business partner and I took extreme measures to ensure that there wasn't a single component in any of our rooms that didn't belong with its respective theme. For example, when we opened our Western Saloon room, we watched movies and shows that were from that era. With that information, we made our saloon look as though it was built right before 1900. To match the theme of the room, we found a working piano from 1900 as well as a working cash register from that era. If there was a game prop that would bring a positive experience to the room, but it didn't fit the time period and theme, then we wouldn't include it in the experience

There are two main reasons we chose to be this detailed. First, we truly want you to feel as though you are in the experience. When you walk into the saloon there is a huge bar right in front of you with old bottles and a cash register from the 1900s. There's a 120-year-old piano in the corner and a wagon wheel light hanging from the ceiling. The wallpaper shimmers gold as a poker table awaits players in the corner. You've gone back a hundred-plus years and entered a whole new world of the wild west, guns, and gambling! The other reason we were detailed with the items inside the room is so that you don't know which items are red herrings and which aren't.

A red herring is something that deceives or diverts attention away from a correct conclusion. For example, if you were in our Egyptian Tomb room and there were a computer on the wall, not only would its presence not make sense in relation to the room, but it would make it too obvious that it is most likely part of a puzzle that needed solved. We didn't want it to be that easy for the individuals who play our rooms to determine what is a part of the game and what is simply a distraction.

One of my favorite examples of a red herring can be found inside our Egyptian Tomb room. This room is, by far, my most treasured experience, as the puzzles are unique and the room, itself, looks just like the inside of an Egyptian Tomb. The ceiling is painted gold, which shines when you enter the room. On one side of the room there are huge columns stretching all the way up the 10-foot ceiling. Every wall is covered with hand painted hieroglyphics that tell the story of the king that lies in the golden sarcophagus. An eight-foot statue of the God Anubis is standing in the corner, guarding the Tomb from any intruders that wish to rob the pharaoh of his treasures (aka you!). It is probably the most visually appealing room—at least to me.

Throughout the game players find blocks that have symbols on them. The other side of the block provides a translation of the symbols to its corresponding letter. On one of the walls in the Tomb there is a rather large ankh, or cross with a looped top, painted on the wall. Painted inside the ankh are four symbols. Players usually don't pay any attention to the ankh painted on the wall in the beginning of the game, mainly because there are so many other distractions in the room from the start. As the production unfolds, players start gathering more and more of these translation blocks. I was watching a group play the Tomb, and around the halfway point, one player started to take notice of the four symbols painted inside the ankh. At this point, the players usually have one or two of the translation blocks that can be used to start decoding. They won't get the required blocks to translate the entire four symbols until later in the game. One person in this group was convinced the four symbols painted on the ankh had to mean something. Each time another block was discovered, this player would grab the block to see if it was one of the missing symbols on the wall. The symbols inside the ankh spell out M-I-K-E. Mike is the other owner of Great Escape Game. This, of course, does nothing to progress game play for the group and only serves as a distraction.

Mike and I wanted to be inside every room. In the Outbreak room pictures of us wearing lab coats and scientist glasses hang on the wall. In the Prison room our names are on the lockers. Just like Alfred Hitchcock liked to be in his own movies, we wanted to be a part of every experience at the Great Escape. Anyway, back to the story about the distracted individual in the Tomb.

The player decoding the letters inside this ankh realizes quickly that MIKE doesn't have any significance in helping them escape the Tomb and play progressed. The team would beat the room with 38 seconds left. However, much time was spent on a meaningless painting in the top corner of the Tomb. In every room, we have at least one red herring to keep the players guessing. Just like real life, there are things that we feel are important but are just distracting us. How many times are we brought off course throughout the day with things that don't matter: our own real-life red herrings?

OBSERVATION 28

Focus on the task at hand.

CHAPTER TWENTY-NINE

Trust Me, I'm an Engineer

"Engineers like to solve problems.
If there are no problems handily available,
they will create their own problems."

—SCOTT ADAMS—

As I have mentioned, the Great Escape Game is located right next to a very large military base. Because of that fact, we see all kinds of different types of professionals play our games. This includes, but is not limited to, personnel that are financial managers, project managers, researchers, and even contract negotiators. But there is one group of professionals that stands out from the pack: the engineers. These individuals think and act a little different from everyone else. Engineers can be known to consider every angle before deciding. This methodical thinking process can serve as a real benefit in several different scenarios; however, sometimes this need to analyze every detail can hinder them. This is especially true in our Bank Vault room. Although this room is our easiest experience with a 50 percent escape rate, it can be a difficult experience for engineers.

Inside the Bank Vault there are many red herrings that take the attention away from the clues the group needs to solve. The main distractions in the room are the different items that have numbers on them. Since it is a bank, there are several posters and financial information that contain numbers throughout the room. One group of engineers spent five minutes trying out random numbers on a lock in the beginning of the game because they all agreed that a poster in the room had to mean something. You may be asking; don't other non-engineers do the same thing? Yes, they do. The difference is that once an engineer gets an idea in his or her head, he or she can find it very hard to stop thinking about it.

Escape rooms have a certain level of depth and difficulty. Within each experience and each puzzle there can be layers of complexity. Usually in the beginning of the game we start players off with unlocking or solving something easy and then the puzzles increase in difficulty as the game goes on. While we aim for the puzzles to be challenging and thought provoking, our goal is not to make them impossible to answer or consist of too many layers. I've noticed that engineers take things to a level so deep that even I don't know how they've arrived at their conclusions.

This was especially true for one group I watched play the Bank Vault room. This group of engineers was doing great in the room; however, about halfway through the hour, progress stopped because of a currency chart hanging on the wall. Convinced it meant something, the group members started doing some advanced math with the money they'd found in the room and the numbers associated with this graph. They, then, started getting numbers from another part of the room and used those digits to calculate it into an equation. After minutes of debating and crunching numbers, they all decided on a four-digit number that they were convinced meant something. They said it out loud to one another to confirm it's the number that they all came up with. They started trying the number on a couple of the locks in the room. At that point, I came over the microphone and said that was the wrong number. The players were shocked, to say the least. One asked me if I was sure the number wasn't right. The engineers then proceeded to explain how they arrived at those numbers. They were speaking loudly, yet I wasn't sure if they were talking to me or to themselves.

After they finished their rather detailed explanation, I came over the microphone to tell them that wasn't the right number and that the posters in the room they were using to get the numbers didn't matter. A different engineer in the room walked over to the poster I was referring to and started to explain to me again from where he got the numbers. For a third time, I explained to the group that the poster in the room was just for looks and wouldn't be used in the game. The group was distraught and didn't like the fact that the artwork chalked full of numbers meant nothing. Some of the players didn't even believe me and continued to calculate. This in-depth analysis is very common with engineer groups. However, these examples aren't supposed to paint engineers as incompetent. In fact, the opposite is true. Some of the fastest escape times have come from engineers.

One group of engineers came in to play their first escape room and rocked it. Four engineers walked in without a reservation and didn't have a preference on which room they played. I talked them into the Egyptian Tomb because it is my favorite room, and it offered some extremely unique puzzles and clues that I felt like they would enjoy and appreciate. I went over the rules and put them in the room. Inside the room there are two game lines that you need to complete to remove the curse and get the treasure. The Tomb is a unique room in the fact that you have everything you need to start both game lines in the room in the first 10-15 minutes. Of course, nobody realizes that they have all the pieces they need in the beginning, which is part of the reason it's my favorite room.

Toward the start of the game the players find an object that they could use to start the second game line of the room. I'd tell you what it is, but then the room would be too easy for you when you come and play it. In almost all the games I've watched, players don't realize that they can use that object, in conjunction with another item they found earlier, to progress through the game. There aren't too many red herrings in each of our experiences; so, when you find something, chances are it can be used to progress you through the game. Engineers usually know this bit of information better than other groups. They look at things in a systematic, logical manner, and if they find an object after opening something, they are convinced it means something and will work towards figuring out what that is.

When one of the players found said object, he knew that it must be used in the room. With the object in hand, he wandered around the Tomb trying to solve its riddle. It didn't take him long to find the component that it linked with, and the puzzle was solved. It was the quickest I've ever seen that puzzle figured out. The remainder of the game was no different than the previous puzzle, and the group ended up passing with 20 minutes left to play. Every step throughout the game was calculated. The desire of this group of engineers to figure things out could almost be felt from the game master room. They were awesome.

OBSERVATION 29

Sometimes, you just have to go all in. If you're wrong, you'll know sooner rather than later.

CHAPTER THIRTY

Three Generations of Fun

*"We are stuck with technology, when what we
really want is just stuff that works."*
−DOUGLAS ADAMS−

As I am writing this book, there are currently three generations of escape rooms. A generation refers to how technologically advanced a room is. A first-generation escape room is dependent on simple devices such as lock boxes and a wide variety of locks. The second- and third-generation rooms add more complicated puzzles that use RFID switches and full automation.

When we first started Great Escape, there wasn't that much technology readily available to us to purchase in the commercial market. We relied heavily on the combination, letter, and keyed locks that you would expect from a first-generation room. Building a room using these types of locks made installation and maintenance easy. One of the benefits of using simple lock-boxes was that if a lock were to break, the staff members would be able to easily replace it with a new one. Another benefit of easy-to-open locks is the level of excitement it can bring to a player and a group. Although opening a lockbox is considered basic, a player does feel some level of accomplishment when he or she gets one open. This is one of the main reasons why we still have first-generation locks in our rooms.

A second-generation escape room starts to introduce reed switches, different types of sensors, audio effects, and props that can be activated with a controller. These tools can help create a better experience for the players by creating more realistic rooms and props. An example of this can be found in our Egyptian Tomb room. In that experience, players find ancient objects that, when placed in certain areas in the room, trigger hidden compartments to open. It's a very exciting way to end the game when everything starts to open at once, including the sarcophagus. A second-generation lock is useful in a room like the Egyptian Tomb, where we try to limit the amount of technology that customers can see to better fit the room's historical theme.

The last type of room is called third generation. There are no padlocks in these rooms. Everything is automated through electronics, computers, and other technology. In theory, generation three rooms should allow for customers to get the most immersive experience. With automation, the computer can control the flow of the game and even make the experience harder or easier in real time if the groups are doing extremely well or poorly. These rooms are usually tremendously expensive to build and maintain.

As a team-building exercise, my employees, my business partner, and I once played a third-generation escape room at another escape room business. In the middle of the game we noticed something on a computer screen was spelled wrong as well as a name of a tool used in the game. After the end of the experience, the game master walked in to talk to us. The gentleman was either the owner or manager, and we started talking about several things. We pointed out the spelling errors, and he informed us it would cost him thousands of dollars to fix that simple error because he would have to redo the entire software program in the room. The room was incredible but having a third-generation room made switching a simple mistake expensive.

Our escape rooms have a good mix of first- and second-generation items. We are always working on changing out some of our first-generation locks and switching them with second-generation items especially if it adds to the experience. Our goal with our escape rooms is to make each experience as realistic as possible while providing the highest level of fun and excitement. Although basic locks serve an important role in the overall experience of an escape room, we do try to eliminate them as often as possible. One of the reasons to replace the first-generation locks is the existence of lock pickers. On rare occasion, we'll have some groups come in, and instead of trying to play the game they spend their time trying to pick the locks. The Tomb is the worst for this type of scenario.

There aren't too many locks in the Egyptian Tomb, but there is one lock that can be picked somewhat easily. This padlock is made to look more than a thousand years old and as a result its locking function is basic. This lock uses letter combinations but there are only four letters per turn dial and if you pulled on it while turning the dials the lock will eventually come apart. This happened once during a game I was watching in which I could tell that an older gentleman was trying to pick the lock. I came over the microphone a couple of times and told him that he didn't have the code for that lock yet. He put the lock down for a moment. Shortly after, he came back to the lock to try once more. I came over the microphone again to tell him that he didn't have the code for the 1,000-year-old lock yet, but he didn't listen to me. He ended up picking the lock, and the group had only been in the room for 10 minutes. The problem with this is that it throws off the entire game. The lock he picked was supposed to be opened towards the end of the game; so, now I must go out of my way to distract the players and lead them down a different path.

The group continued playing the game and came across another box with a lock on it. This box has four numbered dials on it that go from zero to nine. This box won't be opened until past the midway point in the game. Throughout the game the players find certain objects that have numbers on them. The players don't necessarily know that the numbers on these objects go to that four-dial lock, and they won't know the order of the numbers until later in the game. The gentleman that had picked the lock in the beginning of the game picked up this box with the four-dial combination lock on it. The group had found two objects in the game with numbers on them; so, at this point he started to guess the other two numbers and the order in which they would be. There are a lot of combinations to a four dial, 10-digit number lock, ten-thousand combinations to be exact. I didn't pay that much attention to this guy trying to guess the lock because there are so many possible combinations, and even if he did pick a lock earlier in the game, the chances of him picking, or guessing, this lock were slim. About five minutes later he had somehow guessed the lock and opened the box! If his first lock picking didn't mess up the flow of the game, then this second lock-pick really screwed things up.

The group had skipped over a third of the game because of this and now were about to win the game with nearly 25 minutes left. I tried as hard as I could to delay them with the final piece of the game but to no avail. Too much in the room had been skipped, and there was no stopping them. The group ended up passing with 23 minutes left in the game. Not only did the guy not listen to me when I told him to stop playing around with the lock, but he also didn't get a chance to experience half the game. On the rare occasion when these situations occur, I am always worried that after the game the players will be upset because they didn't get to see the entire game as well as the fact that they paid money for an hour experience and only played for half that time. I asked if everyone had fun, to which they replied yes. I didn't want to leave it at that; so, I explained to them that they skipped a lot of things because of the lock picking, and I proceeded to show them how to open the items they skipped. I busted the lock picker's chops a little bit and made sure to be clear, in a playful way, that they skipped half the game because of his lock-picking ability. They all seemed like they were satisfied with the experience; so, I took their end-of-the-game picture and thanked them for coming out.

We have since removed the older lock with a second-generation box that is held together with magnets that can't be picked. It drives me crazy when I see people trying to pick locks, and I'm quick on the microphone to shut it down when I see an attempt being made. The ironic part is that when I play an escape game myself, I find that I am doing anything I can to cheat the system. I can remember two specific times in which I found myself guessing combinations. When the timer is going, the only thing you can think about is escaping. That means with or without following the rules and trying to pick the locks.

OBSERVATION 30

Learning skills can help when technology can't.

CHAPTER THIRTY-ONE

Why We Do
What We Do

"Always leave room for some fun and adventure."
−DANIEL HUIET−

The best part about the escape game business is the fact that people come here to have a good time. When you are in one of our rooms, your phone is put away and you are focused on the only thing that's important at that moment: escaping. People often understand what a company does or how it operates, but they don't always understand why a company exists. At the Great Escape Game our "why" is simple, we want to help individuals escape reality. It's that basic. When individuals go inside our rooms, I don't want them focusing on anything except the tasks associated with escaping the room. That's a big reason we don't allow phones in the room. We are all addicted to our phones, aren't we? Studies have found that people are willing to give up on food, sleep, and even sex rather than lose their internet connection or the ability to check their phone. Think about the last time you went an entire day without your phone. Scary thought, isn't it?

Although you are only locked in our room for an hour instead of all day, the effects are incredible. People actually start talking and interacting with each other. It's the strangest phenomenon you'll ever see in the digital age in which we live. I can't tell you how many groups I've watched that have come out of the rooms and commented on how great it was that everyone was interacting with each other and were off their phones. Playing one of our escape rooms can have the benefit of improving communication between individuals. Sometimes it can mean a whole lot more than that.

I was working late on a Sunday afternoon, when a father and his kids came in to play the Tomb. The family had never played an escape room before, and the young girls were very excited to play the game. The father didn't seem too enthusiastic to be playing an escape room and kind of slouched around the lobby waiting to get this over with. I seemingly dragged the father, against his will, to the Tomb entrance, went over the rules, and put the family into the room. Once inside the pharaoh's Tomb, the young girls started running around the room, searching through everything while giggling in excitement. They were terrible but were having such a great time that I helped them out a little more than normal.

About halfway through, I noticed a change in the father's behavior. This gentleman had not been having any fun from the moment he walked into the lobby. All of the sudden, he was getting more immersed into the experience and became very active in the second half of the game, running around the room trying to unlock the secrets of the pharaoh's Tomb. Initially, the group was not on pace to finish the room, but with the father's newfound enthusiasm, the family was now doing great. The family ended up barely passing the room with less than one minute to spare. I walked into the room and congratulated the family members on their hard-fought victory. They were all ecstatic that they passed.

About a month later, I was at a local Chipotle with my business partner Mike, when I ran into the same guy and his daughters. I don't think he knew who I was while I was standing in line behind him, but I remembered watching his group play the Tomb. He saw me wearing my Great Escape Game t-shirt and asked me if I worked there (I must have left a lasting impression as his game master). I told him that I was the owner. At that moment the father shook my hand and told me that he played the Tomb about a month ago. He said, "In all honesty, I didn't want to play an escape room, but my daughters insisted on going; so, I went. I had so much fun." He went on to tell me that three months ago his wife had filed for divorce. Being inside the escape room was the first time since the filing that he was able to take his mind off of the separation. He gave me the most heartfelt thank you anyone has ever given me. I don't think he realized it, but he was shaking my hand the entire time he was telling me about the divorce. That one hour had meant so much to him. I thought the father was going to cry while standing in line telling me that story, and for a moment I felt as though I might as well. What he experienced was more than just an evening locked in a room with his kids; it was an opportunity to escape reality, and for that short hour that's exactly what happened.

OBSERVATION 31

Have fun as much as you can.
Escape to adventure.

CHAPTER THIRTY-TWO

In Conclusion

"Life's just a bunch of accidents, connected by one perfect end."
—DANIEL TOMAS—

Here we are at the end of our journey together. Throughout this book I have told you about the several different things I've seen while watching more than 1,500 escape rooms: from amazing team leaders to those who wouldn't listen to even our ghost! When I started writing this book, I had watched more than a thousand escape games. At the time of publication, I have watched more than 1,500, and the moments and lessons I have seen will always be with me.

I'd like to end this book by reminding you to always believe in your abilities. Never use words to bring someone down. Recognize those in your life who are the superstars. Know your strengths, but also understand your weaknesses. Never judge a book or a person by its cover. Learn, evolve, adapt, and listen. Let go of your pride and admit when you don't know something. Lift people up in your life, and never stop being bold. Live this adventure known as life to the fullest. Finally, and most importantly, turn off your phone and give yourself at least an hour to escape reality!

Why I Decided to Write This Book

In January of 2016 I was working a 9-5 job, while teaching college-level business courses online. I also was running several businesses in the wedding industry, offering DJ, photo booth, lighting, party bus, and other services. The last thing on my mind was starting another business or getting involved in another time-consuming venture. That all changed when I played my first escape room. I originally heard about the concept when visiting my aunt and uncle in Germany in 2014. Unfortunately, I was traveling alone at the time, and the local escape room website recommended bringing a group of people to help; so, I decided to pass on the experience. That was a huge mistake! After returning from my trip to Germany, I forgot all about the escape room concept that I was so eager to try. At the end of 2015 I discovered an escape room business close to where I lived, and I booked my first game with a group of friends. I had no clue what to expect when those doors locked behind me, but I would soon find out how much I loved playing the game. The scenario we picked gave us an hour to try to escape and three clues. After what seemed like only 10 minutes, we had successfully completed the room in 55 minutes, leaving us just five minutes to catch our breaths. I was hooked!

A month later, I booked another escape room with a few friends. It was another tense yet successful outing. We somehow managed to beat the hour timer again with a similar five minutes left to spare. My group of friends and I decided to go out for dinner and drinks at a nearby pizza joint to celebrate. While at dinner, my now business partner, Mike, looked at me and asked, "Why don't we make our own escape room?" A light bulb turned on in my head, and by the end of the very next night, we had drawn up our first scenario at my home. We stayed up the entire night and determined all of the puzzles and clues that would be included in our first escape room. In a short four months, we had opened our escape room business, featuring two rooms: the Bank Vault and The Virus Outbreak. We were new to the escape game world and had a lot to learn about how to structure rooms and the puzzles that went inside them. More importantly, we had a lot to learn about the people who were about to play our escape rooms.

Initially, we never gave any thought to the fact that various individuals would act and react differently to the elements in each room and the other players participating with them. It only took about a month for us to notice the different behavioral patterns within the diverse groups of people that came into our business. As time went on we started paying very close attention to even the smallest action taken by an individual playing a game. We noticed that a sizable portion of players fell into certain roles, and if there wasn't something in the room that accommodated a player's specific skill set, he or she would get frustrated, annoyed, and sometimes even bored. We certainly didn't want anyone to leave our rooms having an unpleasant experience. Therefore, a change was in order after being in business for only a short two months. We transformed several elements in the rooms to appeal to the wider variety of skill sets. This helped ensure that there was something for everyone in each room. As we continued to build rooms, we kept this important consideration in mind: each room would need to have an assortment of puzzles and clues that would appeal to the multitude of different aptitudes. With careful attention to detail, over the span of 12 months we built six rooms that encompassed a collection of diverse puzzles and clues to match our audience's talents. Over a span of three years, I had the pleasure of watching more than 1,500 escape room experiences at my business. Hopefully, the experiences that I have shared in this book provided you with as much enjoyment and insight into human behavior as it has for me!

I decided to write this book primarily for two reasons. The first is that I've always been passionate about communication and leadership. The behaviors I have witnessed in the escape rooms fall in line with those two subjects perfectly. As an entrepreneur I have come to realize that the success of a business relies heavily on leadership and communication skills from the owners, managers, and employees. Without these important and critical skills, a business can find itself imploding. This failure to communicate not only has an impact on business and everyday life but also makes an enormous difference in whether you will win playing an escape room. The second reason I decided to write this book was due to popular demand. I've had dozens of individuals come out of our escape rooms and mention to me that they were curious to know what we see when watching the games. Feeling a personal duty to not disappoint my customers and a burning desire to share what I witnessed watching more than 1,500 groups of players, I decided to pick up my pen, or in this case laptop, and begin writing. This wasn't for me but for everyone out there who wanted to know what I saw. As the expression goes: Ask, and you shall receive.

Made in the USA
Monee, IL
24 April 2024

57416362R00100